The Writer's Workbook

Edited by

Jenny Newman, Edmund Cusick and Aileen La Tourette

*School of Media, Critical and Creative Arts,
Liverpool John Moores University*

ARNOLD

A member of the Hodder Headline Group
LONDON

Co-published in the United States of America by
Oxford University Press Inc., New York

First published in Great Britain in 2000 by
Arnold, a member of the Hodder Headline Group,
338 Euston Road, London NW1 3BH

http://www.arnoldpublishers.com

Co-published in the United States of America by
Oxford University Press Inc.,
198 Madison Avenue, New York, NY10016

The advice and information in this book are believed to be true and
accurate at the date of going to press, but neither the author[s] nor the publisher
can accept any legal responsibility or liability for any errors or omissions.

British Library Cataloguing in Publication Data
A catalogue record for this book is available from the British Library

Library of Congress Cataloging-in-Publication Data
A catalog record for this book is available from the Library of Congress

ISBN 0 340 75999 2 (hb)
ISBN 0 340 76001 X (pb)

1 2 3 4 5 6 7 8 9 10

Production Editor: Wendy Rooke
Production Controller: Fiona Byrne
Cover Design: Terry Griffiths

Typeset in 10/12 Palatino by Phoenix Photosetting, Chatham, Kent
Printed and bound in by MPG Books Ltd, Bodmin, Cornwall

What do you think about this book? Or any other Arnold title?
Please send your comments to feedback.arnold@hodder.co.uk

CONTENTS

Part Three: Branching out

ABOUT THE EDITORS

Edmund Cusick has collaborated with Ann Gray jointly to publish a volume of poetry, *Gronw's Stone* (Headland, 1997). In 1998 he won the Housman Poetry Prize and was a runner-up for the Bridport Poetry Prize. He is currently editing an anthology of contemporary women's poetry. He is course leader for the BA in Imaginative Writing at Liverpool John Moores Centre for Writing.

As writer-in-residence at HMP Ford, **Aileen La Tourette** taught creative writing and drama across the prison community. She has also taught creative writing to *The Big Issue* in London, on the Antioch University MA programme, and for the Arvon Foundation. She has published numerous poems and short stories, two novels, *Nuns and Mothers* (Virago, 1984) and *Cry Wolf* (Virago, 1986), and has had many plays on radio. She now teaches on the BA, MA and PhD programmes at Liverpool John Moores Centre for Writing.

Jenny Newman is the editor of *The Faber Book of Seductions* (Faber and Faber, 1988) and co-editor of *Women Talk Sex: Autobiographical Writing about Sex, Sexuality and Sexual Identity* (Scarlet Press, 1992). She has also written two novels, *Going In* (Penguin, 1995) and *Life Class* (Chatto and Windus, 1999), and many articles on contemporary British writing. She is currently Head of Liverpool John Moores Centre for Writing.

ABOUT THE CONTRIBUTORS

Dymphna Callery has an MA in Writing Studies and over 10 years' experience of teaching drama and writing in higher education. Her poetry collection, *What She Said and What She Did*, was published by Headland in 1997, and she has had five plays performed in theatre and on radio, including her recent adaptation of *Thérèse Raquin* at the Unity Theatre, Liverpool, in 1999. She currently teaches in the Drama Department at Liverpool John Moores University.

Gladys Mary Coles has published eight volumes of poetry, including *The Glass Menagerie* (Duckworth, 1992) and *Leafburners* (Duckworth, 1986). Her major prizes include the Aberystwyth Open, the National Poetry Competition, the Scottish and Cardiff Internationals, and a Welsh Arts Council writer's award. Her work is anthologized by Faber, Cassell, Virago, Forward Prizes and in *Twentieth Century Anglo-Welsh Poetry* (Seren, 1997).

James Friel is the author of *Left of North* (Macmillan, 1989), winner of a Betty Trask award; *Taking the Veil* (Macmillan, 1990); and *Careless Talk* (Macmillan, 1994), which was nominated for the *Mail on Sunday* John Llewellyn Rhys Prize and a Welsh Arts Council bursary. He also writes for screen and radio. His adaptations of David Hare's *Saigon* and Charlotte Brontë's *Villette* were broadcast on BBC Radio 4 in 1999, and his adaptation of Balzac's *Cousin Bette* will be broadcast in 2000.

Dave Jackson is a freelance screenwriter and singer/songwriter. He has a BA in Imaginative Writing and an MA in Screenwriting, and won a Lynda La Plante bursary in 1996. He is currently developing two screenplays for independent producers. He has also sung with and written songs for post-punk indie bands The Room, Benny Profane and Dust. With these bands he has also released six LPs and a number of EPs and singles. Between 1980 and 1990 he recorded six John Peel sessions and toured in Europe, the US and Canada. He still writes and performs with Dead Cowboys, who have just recorded a mini-album of 'twisted roots' music.

PREFACE

There are many ways of becoming a successful writer, but none of them happens overnight. It takes talent, determination and luck. Today's writers may benefit from imaginative publishing houses, technology, new opportunities in film, television and the digital media, global links such as the world wide web, and other new directions in the arts world. But funding for the arts is shrinking, and publishing, film and television companies are increasingly market-driven. Without advice and support, new writers can find themselves at a loss.

In both Britain and the United States, universities have begun to play a major role in the development of new writing. At Liverpool John Moores Centre for Writing we offer a three-year course leading to a BA in Imaginative Writing. *The Writer's Workbook* is based on our programme, and we strongly recommend that you work through the chapters in order.

This is a book for people determined to write. Only if you engage with its ideas, test its tenets and follow the exercises will you give yourself the chance to develop and expand your talent. We hope you enjoy it.

ACKNOWLEDGEMENTS

We would like to thank our colleagues past and present whose inspiration and support have helped us evolve our ideas. We would also like to thank all the students who, through their insight and enthusiasm, have enabled us to develop and refine the methods described in this book.

Part One:
Exploring

1 OBSERVATION AND DISCOVERY

Edmund Cusick

INTRODUCTION

Your own life is the first source of your writing. You gather material by paying attention to the world around you. Otherwise, you may ultimately find yourself writing stories which are recycled versions of characters, situations and events you have seen on television or read about in other books.

Your writing material comes from things you have seen, heard and felt. Daily life surrounds us with a barrage of impressions that may at first seem irrelevant to, or a distraction from, writing. Yet this can be the grit which, when panned and sifted, yields the grains of gold which inspire poetry, stories or screenplays. Becoming a writer will involve changes in the way you approach life and in your attitude to your surroundings and everyday experience.

All writing is founded on effective description – the basic literary draughtsmanship that allows you to express your sense impressions clearly. Whether you are writing about inner-city tower blocks, Caribbean islands or medieval monks, this is the art that makes your scenes and characters real to a reader. Description is founded on observation. One of the best ways of developing the art of articulating physical impressions is to practise it, mentally or in a notebook, in your daily surroundings.

OBSERVATION

Absorb the idea that as a writer you are never off duty. Make it your goal to turn dead time – while waiting for a bus or train, or standing in a queue – into creative time by practising observation. (When in a new place, first look around you, then close your eyes and listen.) Train your imaginative powers by challenging yourself to put each new situation to some creative use. Among the silt you will find gold, that moment when you say, 'I can use that'.

For many writers who draw their subjects from the contemporary world, daily life may provide locations, ideas for characters and even plots. Many forms of writing depend on effective description, drawing ultimately on sensory experience. A fantasy writer may set her sword and sorcery novels in worlds far removed from this one, yet her accounts of warriors and knights might depend on her close study of Samurai weapons seen in a museum, medieval castles explored on holiday, or the detailed descriptions of horses gathered at races or on a farm.

A notebook is a vital tool for any writer. Just as a photographer always carries a camera, so a writer always carries a notebook. Buy one small enough to fit in your pocket. Use it to note down brief descriptions, first impressions, snatches of conversation. Your notes on the spot will carry the freshness of immediate observation, which will carry on into later reworkings. It can be helpful to buy a disposable camera. A photographic print will always show things that were not part of your mental picture, but which might prove useful later.

Professional writers may spend years gathering material. Even without a specific goal in mind you can be a magpie, collecting vicarious experience whenever you can. Ask questions. Most people carry tales of the strangest, the most frightening, the most exciting thing that has ever happened to them, and many are willing to share their stories. See Chapter 15 for further advice on this kind of research.

THE NEWSAGENT

We are surrounded with written stories as well as oral ones. Many authors turn to daily newspapers for raw material. While some – tabloid newspapers and chat magazines specializing in human interest stories – are obvious sources of plots, the science, crime or archaeology column may equally yield the germ of an idea. With a little imagination, frag-ments of stories can also be found in the personal columns, the items for sale, the situations vacant.

Exploit new experiences. Mix and match. You are unlikely ever to get a whole package – a work of art – presented to you on a plate, and if you did your opportunities as a writer would be limited. You may take a line of dialogue you have overheard and change it, or put it in the mouth of one of your characters; take an anecdote and use it as part of a plot; put a person you have seen on a train in a place you visited years ago. Coleridge referred to the imagination as a harmonizing and synthesizing power that takes disparate elements and makes of them a satisfying whole. All writing is based on this mosaic quality to some extent. But the material must first be gathered.

PEOPLE-WATCHING

People-watching can be fascinating and most of us do it half-consciously. Casual observation should become an ever stronger part of your writer's life, wherever you are. There is a place, too, for detective work – deliberate, systematic observation. Remember, though, to exercise tact, common sense and discretion at all times. Observation should never become an invasion of someone else's privacy. It is surprising how many new writers, caught up in the excitement of gathering material, have forgotten basic rules of common sense and found themselves in embarrassing situations.

- *Do* go where large numbers of people gather and move around: for example, to motorway services, railway stations and large supermarkets.
- *Don't* go where people mainly socialize, or sit still – waiting rooms, for example. Like all animals, people have a sixth sense that tells them if they are being watched and this is far more active when they are stationary and at leisure than when they are involved in some complex activity. Intense observation in pubs or cafés is tempting, but will invariably get you spotted by the object of your observation and could lead to unfortunate misunderstandings.
- *Never* take out your notebook in the presence of someone you are observing – what would you do if you saw someone making notes about you?
- *Never* follow people, no matter how interesting they may be. One observation must be enough.
- *Do* cultivate the art of rapid observation – from hairstyle to shoes, through hand luggage, clothes, complexion, jewellery and expression – in a single glance. It will come with practice.
- *Do* learn the knack of invisibility – of blending in with the background.
- *Do* use indirect ways of observation – through reflections in shop windows, or CCTV television screens. You can stare at these for a minute at a time without anyone taking offence.

DISCOVERY

Here are some practical ideas for developing your powers of observation. Select those which are most helpful to you as a writer, and build them into your daily life. If you get into the habit of observation, even the material that you do not use will sharpen your skills of observation, and serve to lay the foundations of future writing.

- Buy an all-day bus pass or train pass and spend the day travelling with your notebook.

- Go to a place you visit every day. Look up to rooftop level, down to the floor or pavement and examine details. Try to spot three things you have never noticed.

- Write a set of instructions for a journey you take regularly, without mentioning street names, or directions such as right or left. Imagine you were instructing someone to take the same route, navigating only by visible landmarks. You may think you know the route backwards, but will probably find you have to walk it again, discovering new things.

- Buy a different newspaper. If you read a local paper try the *Financial Times* or the *Wall Street Journal*; if you read the *Guardian* or the *New Yorker*, try the *Star* or the *National Inquirer*. Buy two magazines you have never even looked at, let alone considered buying: *Coarse Fishing*, *Vogue*, *People*, *True Confessions*, *Seventeen*, *Tattoo World*, *Prediction*, *Caravanning Monthly*, *Loaded*. Take an item from each of the three publications: say, an item for sale from one, a picture from another, a storyline from a third. Work them together into a story, poem, or idea for a play.

- Use the whole of one such publication – letters page, small ads, horoscope even – to think yourself into the mind of a regular reader and consider how you could use such a character in your writing.

- Go to a supermarket and pick up as many discarded itemized till receipts as you can find. Read them and choose the most interesting. Examine the list of items bought and use all your powers of deduction. What, do you think, was the customer's age, sex, occupation? Were they buying only for themselves, or for someone else as well? Consider everything – the time they shopped, the day of the week, the method of payment. From the clues of lifestyle, income, diet and habits gained from the receipt, construct an identity for your mystery shopper.

- Go to a bus or railway station, an airport or ferry terminal. Observe groups of people meeting or saying goodbye. Deduce or imagine who they are and what their lives contain. Ask yourself, if these people were characters in my story, what would happen next?

- At the supermarket till, glance discreetly at the purchases of other shoppers. Do they fit the picture you would build of the person, or do they surprise you?

- Find a place where you will be safe, comfortable and undisturbed. Take two minutes to listen by closing your eyes. If you find this embarrassing, you could always pretend to be asleep. Observe the different textures and layers of sound – from noises in the distance, continuous background sound and occasional interruptions to small sounds nearby. On a bus or a local train you will have far more chance of overhearing a whole conversation than you would by occupying a fixed position on a street. On the other hand, following a conversation is likely to make you oblivious to other sounds. In populated areas, it is safest to do this in twos or threes, with only one person listening at a time, the others remaining silent.

* Set yourself the task of writing about something that interests you but about which you have no first-hand experience: for example, an event in another time or country. Learn everything you can through TV documentaries, books or the internet. Talk to people who may have more knowledge. Read first-hand accounts and try to find an imaginative point of entry to the story – perhaps through a character with whom you can identify. Write a piece about the event in the first person.

* Make a journey or extended field trip, perhaps as part of a writing group, to a place which is likely to yield inspiration: the Rockies or the Welsh mountains, Stonehenge or the Painted Desert, the City of London or the Redwood Highway – somewhere radically different from the place where you work or study. Immersion in a creative purpose for a day, or a whole weekend, can be a boost to your writing and can give you the chance to share inspiration with fellow writers. Through cameras and notebooks, practise seeing places through different eyes.

2 KEEPING A WRITER'S JOURNAL

Jenny Newman

INTRODUCTION

The terms 'journal' and 'diary' both have their roots in older words for day and many writers use them interchangeably. Both words suggest a strong link with habit. Keeping a writer's journal, or diary, over months and years gives you the time and space to pay attention to your creative processes, and is a sign of your commitment to being a writer. It can become exciting, comforting and fundamentally helpful – both when you write it and days, or years, later.

Note the following quotation from Kafka, copied by the American poet Allen Ginsberg into his journal, 25 February 1912: 'Hold fast to the diary from today on! Write regularly! Don't surrender! Even if no salvation should come, I want to be worthy of it every moment.'[1]

At the start of a recent workshop a group of MA Writing students took out their writer's journals, which included:

- an artist's sketchbook
- a box filled with 5" × 3" cards in alphabetical order
- a pocket camera
- a spiral notebook
- a shoe box filled with swatches of material, old menus and postcards
- an audio cassette
- a ring binder with dividers between different projects
- a padlocked cash box filled with pieces of paper
- a floppy disk.

The kind of journal you keep is a question of choice. The only kind best avoided is the diary divided into days of the week. If you decide to buy a notebook, we recommend that you choose one small enough to fit in your bag or pocket and a larger one to keep at home. The small notebook can be used when you are on the move and need to note fleeting impressions. If this seems like a chore, remember the words of Thoreau: 'The writer who postpones the recording of his thoughts uses an iron which has cooled to burn a hole with.'[2]

Take time when choosing your large notebook to find one that feels right. Whatever your chosen journal, it should give you room enough to expand and to hold, for example, cuttings, photographs, letters or whatever other sorts of memorabilia you find interesting. Choose one of a good enough quality to last, but not too beautiful to write in. Remember: there is no right or wrong way of keeping a journal. Its only role is to help your writing.

DIFFERENT JOURNALS

There are as many sorts of journals as there are writers. For a wealth of inspiration, read some famous examples. Not only do the journals of, for example, Virginia Woolf, Allen Ginsberg, Katherine Mansfield, Franz Kafka, Marion Milner, Anaïs Nin and May Sarton let you into the secrets of creative problem solving, but they are gripping works in their own right. Authors' collected letters (for example, those of John Keats and D. H. Lawrence) and notebooks (see the notebooks of Henry James) can also give valuable insight into the writing process.

Some writers prefer to subdivide their journals into sections, or even into different books, while others find more stimulus when diverse items rub shoulders. The choice is yours. What follows are some descriptions of different kinds of journals, plus a writing exercise for each to get you started.

The artist's sketchbook

Numbed by habit and overloaded with information, we often fail to notice the uniqueness of our surroundings. Pausing to jot down what you see, smell, feel, taste or overhear helps to reawaken your senses. You do not have to note down everything around you: it is more helpful to focus on how you perceive it. As you already know from Chapter 1, 'Observation and discovery', the moment you record a perception you start giving it a structure and organizing its details.

Once you become aware of how you apprehend the world, you can start choosing the kinds of perceptions you wish to cultivate. As Anaïs Nin wrote in Diary VI: 'Every moment you can choose what you wish to see, observe, or record. It is your choice. So you create the total aspect according to your vision. We have a right to select our vision of the world.'[3]

Reawakening your senses

This exercise sharpens sensory awareness and can be useful as a way of 'limbering up', or triggering or unblocking the imagination. This example focuses on the often-neglected sense of touch, but it can be adapted to apply to each of the senses in turn. The lists in your journal become a kind of imagery bank on which to draw in your writing.

- In the middle of a blank page, write down a list of half a dozen of the objects/things you most dislike touching (e.g. liver, blood, cobwebs).
- To the left of this list, write another list of adjectives or words which tell something more about the objects you dislike touching (e.g. the texture, feel, specific kind or type).
- To the right of the list write another list of verbs which will further illuminate/add meaning to the objects and why you dislike touching them. These verbs should be very exact and energetic.
- Now think of what each item on your list resembles/reminds you of – create a simile or metaphor. This is the important leap into imagery.
- Following the same procedure, make another list of the objects/things you most like to touch (e.g. velvet or cat's fur).
- Take one of your tactile images and use it as the starting point of a poem or story. Incorporate two more of your new images somewhere in the piece of writing. The images can perhaps be the modes or hubs around which the piece is structured (and act as symbols) or alternatively they might be used simply to enhance vividness and originality.[4]

The exercise bar

Anaïs Nin said that 'Writing ... as one practices the piano every day keeps one nimble, and then when the great moments of inspiration come, one is in good form, supple and smooth.'[5] Or, to change the metaphor, journal keeping is like stretches for the athlete, or a place to work out and keep supple. Many writers advise making a date with your journal each day and making sure you keep it. Or you can use a pocket-sized cassette recorder to record your thoughts while, for instance, you are travelling to work, and transcribe those you wish to keep at the end of the day.

Morning pages

Rise half an hour or even an hour earlier than you normally do and, without talking or reading the newspaper, start writing whatever words come into your head. These morning pages, which should not be re-read, are invaluable in fostering a tendency to cast the experiences of the day ahead into words, and to transform the raw material of life into fictional shape.[6]

The playground

Although you need to cultivate your analytical side and study a range of techniques in your chosen form, there are times when it can inhibit your writing. 'Writer's block' sometimes results from straining too hard for effect, or from a fear of being judged by either an inner or an outer critic. This fear can make the pen or word processor freeze mid-sentence, or keep you away from your desk, or even take away the desire to write. To stop yourself from becoming self-conscious or overcritical of your early drafts, you need a place where you can play unobserved and gain the insight into your feelings which is essential for a writer.

When you use your journal for this purpose it is best to write without worrying about grammar or spelling. Even when not blocked, you need the space to take intellectual and creative risks, to doodle or daydream, to rediscover your voice and to experiment with points of view, and this is not the time for meticulous editing. Brenda Ueland urges writers to 'keep a slovenly, headlong, impulsive, honest diary'.[7] By writing the first thoughts that enter your mind, you will not get trapped by what bores you.

But remember that if, like Henry James, you 'take a piece of paper into your confidence',[8] it is best not to show it to your friends – or only under very special circumstances.

Awkward, quick and insolent

Write fast for 10 minutes. You may record your impressions of the day, or stay with a particular subject, or just write what comes into your head. As Brenda Ueland puts it, 'You will go straight to the point – be awkward, quick and insolent.'[9] Remember that you are free to write the worst rubbish in the world, so do not censor yourself and do not worry about grammar and punctuation. To quote Ueland again, 'Be careless, reckless! Be a lion, be a pirate!'[10] Write nonsense words if you feel like it and do not stop if you get stuck; just write the same words over again until new words come.

The store cupboard

You can use your journal for recording what Henry James referred to in his notebook as 'the germ of a story';[11] or for useful jottings, dreams, ideas and visions; snippets of dialogue and images you are currently unable to develop. And if you record these when feeling energetic or inspired you can, like James, use your journal to reflect on them over time, to work out suitable narrative strategies, and to turn your ideas into a work of art when the moment comes. Thus your journal will become an aid to memory, a record and a personal archive. Some of these 'germs' will grow and others will wither and drop away as no longer important.

Spy notebook

Go somewhere out of your usual routine – a wrestling match, sushi bar, art gallery, circus or marshalling yard – with a small journal as your 'spy notebook'. Read the notes on people watching in Chapter 1, 'Observation and discovery'. Write down everything that you see and overhear. Take photographs. Eavesdrop shamelessly.

The timetable

When the Victorian novelist Anthony Trollope began a new book, he prepared a diary, divided it into weeks, and kept it for the period he had allowed himself for the completion for the work. In it he entered, day by day, the number of pages he had written, so that if at times he 'slipped into idleness for a day or two, the record of that idleness has been there, staring me in the face'.[12]

Although few contemporary novelists are as disciplined and productive as Trollope, it is useful to know how long you spend on your writing and how long you postpone it, by keeping a faithful record of what and when you write. Over time this will help you to plan your day, your week and your year, and to reshape it around the times and activities which help your writing most.

You may, if you wish, write down a list of goals and measure your progress towards them. Try to make them achievable rather than wildly ambitious plans for instant success. Remember that once you begin to take your writing seriously, you have the rest of your life to reach them, though that lifelong commitment needs to be reflected at the level of each month, week and – ideally – day.

If you regularly enter writing competitions you will need to keep a record of what you have sent where, the closing date, and what date the results are announced, so that your work may be released to send to a magazine, or to other competitions.

> **Highs and lows**
>
> Pin a timetable over your desk, noting the high spots and low spots in your writing, recording when and where and, if possible, why they happened. Look for patterns.

The reader's log

Being a writer means endless, impassioned and meticulous reading, and every writer's journal is also a reader's journal.

When you start reading in a certain way that is already the beginning of your writing. You are learning what you admire and you are learning to love other writers. The love of other writers is an important first step.[13]

It is crucial to learn how to read a book not only once for pleasure, but several times for technique. Keep a record of what you have read, with notes on style, structure, plot devices or characterization. Copy out lines or paragraphs from your favourite authors. Read writers on writing, and collect those remarks that seem to illuminate the business of being an author. After a while you will find you are assembling your own writing manual, to turn to when you need guidance, or wish to 'raise your game' in terms of technical achievement.

> **Putting on the style**
>
> Copy into your journal or on to your word processor a paragraph from the work of a writer you admire and from whom you would like to learn. Taking a piece of your work in progress, cast it syllable for syllable in the form of that paragraph. The sense of your work will be different from that of your chosen author, but you will have temporarily donned their sentence lengths and the rhythms of their prose.

The factory floor

Some journals are devoted to one piece of work in progress and form a chronological account of the inspiration which nourishes it, and the technical challenges encountered and overcome. As Virginia Woolf used part of her journal for the writing exercises which developed her revolutionary style and methods of characterization, so you too need a place to plan creative tasks, refine your technique, and analyse work in progress and put it through different drafts. Or your journal might be a fishing net, in which you, like Woolf, watch for the arrival of an idea like a 'fin passing far out'.[14] This was her first intimation of *The Waves*, so she could not convey precisely what it meant. But on completing the novel five years later, she wrote in her diary for that night: 'I mean that I have netted that fin in the waste of water which appeared to me over the marshes out of my window at Rodmell when I was coming to an end of To the Lighthouse.'[15]

Question your characters

Write a two-page dialogue between you and one of the characters in your current work of fiction. You may, for example, ask questions about his/her desires, ambitions and feelings towards the other characters, and the events of the plot. This exercise is particularly useful when a character is refusing to come to life.

The sister arts

If you suffer from writer's block, turning for inspiration to another medium may reignite your creative spark. Build a collection of inspiring music on CD or cassette, or assemble photographs of your favourite sculptures. Look out for visits from theatre companies and dance troupes, or visit an art gallery. Many pictures tell a story, or trigger ideas by serving as a symbol of a hidden self.

For some writers dreams are an irrelevance, while others see them as a gateway into their unconscious. For them, dreams are naturally creative, communicating symbols which can feed into their art. Some of the greatest works of imagination, especially in the Gothic and fantasy genres, have allegedly been inspired by dreams: Horace Walpole's *The Castle of Otranto*, S. T. Coleridge's 'Kubla Khan', Mary Shelley's *Frankenstein*, R. L. Stevenson's *Dr Jekyll and Mr Hyde* and George MacDonald's *Lilith*.

Dream catcher

Keep a notebook beside your bed for a month. Write in it on waking, even in the middle of the night, and even if you cannot remember any dreams. Your memory of your dreams will almost certainly improve.

The word hoard

Like people, words are obliged to relate to their next-door neighbours, taking their colour from – or arguing with – the company they keep. But each word has a history of its own and its definition(s) and status can change dramatically across the centuries. It is the writer's job to consider not only a word's current meaning, but also its origin and history. Thus every writer becomes a linguist.

Dictionary visit

- Decide on the central image or symbol of your work in progress and narrow it down to a single word. Find that word in the 24-volume *Oxford English Dictionary*, which is the most extensive in the world (modern English draws words from languages as diverse as Arabic, Sanskrit, Dutch, Japanese and Gaelic). Note your word's origin, its etymology and any outmoded or abandoned usages.
- Write a one-paragraph biography of your word.
- Now consult some dictionaries of myth and legend – for example, African, Greek, Hindu or Breton. Does your word crop up? And does the narrative structure of your one-paragraph biography, or the narrative structure of your work in progress, echo any of the myths?

IN CONCLUSION

Some methods of keeping a journal are relatively recent. Others were in use before the Middle Ages. Doubtless writers in the third millennium will come to depend upon systems which have not yet been invented. The important thing is to experiment until you find the best way for you, and then make sure that you use it regularly. Good luck!

Notes

1 Quoted in Robin Hemley, *Turning Life into Fiction* (Story Press, Cincinnati, 1994).
2 Quoted in Hemley, *Turning Life into Fiction*.
3 Quoted in Tristine Rayner, *The New Diary: How to Use a Journal for Self Guidance and Expanded Creativity* (Angus and Robertson, London, 1986).
4 Adapted from an exercise by Gladys Mary Coles in Susan Sellers (ed.), *Taking Reality by Surprise: Writing for Pleasure and Publication* (Women's Press, London, 1991).
5 Quoted in Raynor, *The New Diary*.
6 Adapted from advice given by Dorothea Brande, *Becoming a Writer* (Macmillan, London, 1986 edn.).
7 Brenda Ueland, *If You Want to Write: Releasing Your Creative Spirit* (Element Books, Shaftesbury, Dorset, 1991).
8 See F. O. Matthiessen and Kenneth B. Murdock (eds.), *The Notebooks of Henry James* (University of Chicago Press, Chicago, 2000).
9 Ueland, *If You Want to Write*.

10 Ueland, *If You Want to Write*.
11 Matthiessen and Murdock, *Notebooks*.
12 Quoted in Susan Shaughnessy, *Meditations for Writers* (HarperCollins, London, 1993).
13 Tess Gallagher, quoted in Amber Coverdale Sumrall (ed.), *Write to the Heart* (The Crossing Press, Freedom, Calif., 1992).
14 Leonard Woolf (ed.), *A Writer's Diary: Being Extracts from the Diary of Virginia Woolf* (Harcourt Brace, New York, 1953).
15 Woolf, *A Writer's Diary*.

3 THE WORKSHOP

Edmund Cusick

WHY JOIN A WORKSHOP?

Writing can be a lonely business. In order to write, even if it is for the collaborative worlds of film or television, you need a degree of solitude. Yet to have some company is an advantage. As a writer, you need readers. Unless your work makes it from the drawer or the computer file to delight another person it is, in a sense, wasted. After all, the reason you want to write is because you feel you have something to say, stories that are worth telling.

As a writer who wishes to improve your work, you need critics. Not carping antagonistic fault finders, but people who know about literature because they care about it. The best people to do this are those who are themselves embarked on the lifelong apprenticeship that is writing. Encouragement can be in short supply as you begin a writing career. It is an axiom of writing that every successful writer begins with rejection slips. Rejection is base camp – the point from which all writers, including many of your own heroes and heroines, set out before they reached the summit. Being part of a group where others have gone through the same process – and begun to make their way up to the summit – can be a huge help.

Encouragement

In your journal, write the most helpful responses to your work you have had so far. They may have been detailed analyses received on a course, an expression of faith in you by someone whose judgement you trust, or someone telling you that they were gripped or entertained by your work. How have they influenced what you have written?

Your writing has strengths and it has weaknesses. To dream of writing the perfect piece straight off is like prospecting in the hope of finding not just a nugget, but a piece of gold which is already miraculously formed in the shape of a ring. The gold – the first rush of inspiration – is only the starting point. Writing is as much about reforging, reworking and redrafting as it is about a flash of blinding inspiration.

Much of the hammering out you do on your own, but all our work has faults and no one sees their own blind spots. They are like the letters of the word 'mountains' across a map. No matter how tough and self-critical you try to be, many of the faults in your own writing will remain invisible to you. You will always benefit from someone who can give you an informed opinion of how your work may be improved. Equally, you need readers, and critics, to tell you what you are doing right.

Investigation

If you could get informed advice on one aspect of your writing, what would it be? Write down one area you are unsure about in your writing. If you had to choose one piece of your own work to receive expert help on, which would it be and why?

Criticism is not a magic wand guaranteed to make your work perfect. Your critics may simply be wrong. They are, however, always worth listening to. If you keep getting a similar response from different readers, then the chances are they have seen something which you have missed.

In a successful workshop, something else will happen. As you devote yourself singlemindedly to other people's work, struggling to think not only of what may need correction but how you would correct it, you will be honing your own critical skill, your gift for literary problem solving: sharpening your nose for the right word, the right rhythm, the best sentence structure. When you return to your own work, you will be a better writer for it.

PREPARATION FOR FEEDBACK

Before you look at each other's work, it is a good idea to look at some published writing. This gets your eye in for what works and what does not, and reminds you of the standards you are trying to attain. If you try to establish the things you value in a piece of writing before you look at each other's, you will find it easier to be objective and precise.

> **Reading for technique**
>
> Take a poem or story. Read it and let everyone comment on one feature which is well done and one which could be improved. It can be interesting to begin with a piece which, though published, seems full of faults, frustrating, difficult, or unpleasant: controversy is good for discussion, and it is sometimes easier to find things to say about work you dislike than work you admire!
>
> Once you have looked at some published work, go round the group to see if you can come up with a list of features which most people agree are good qualities or faults in writing. You may not find agreement, but the discussion will itself begin to clarify the task facing the workshop.

CRITICISM AND FEEDBACK

There are many different ways of handling feedback on writing, but it is a good idea to agree in advance what your method will be, so that everyone feels that they are being treated fairly. Workshops are opportunities to learn, not arenas for praise or condemnation. Always aim to describe individual features of the work, rather than attempting to pronounce a final verdict – like Roman emperors at the games or ice-skating judges. Make sure that everyone who speaks finds one thing that is done well and one thing that could be done better.

In an important sense, all work submitted is work in progress – it is part of your development as a writer. It is far more useful to have a weakness in your style identified – even though this is temporarily painful to your ego – and to correct it, than to be met with a row of happy faces telling you that everything you write is wonderful, in the hope that you will, literally, return the compliment. Criticism should be constructive and specific. If you identify what you think is a weakness, you should work out how this weakness could be remedied. By doing this you are developing the same skills of critical editing and problem solving that you will in turn apply to your own work. Listening closely to other people's work is vital to the development of your own.

There is no place in a workshop for destructive criticism. Comments which sum up the work in a negative way without offering a creative solution are not competent criticisms, and derive from a lazy attitude and a lack of commitment to what a workshop can achieve.

Examples of unhelpful criticism:

'I loved it' 'I didn't like it' ' It's really you' 'I don't know what to say' 'Uh ... pass'

'It's got this feel to it' 'I enjoyed it, but I couldn't say why'

Examples of helpful criticism:

'I liked the way you got into the main character's head – she was really convincing – but I found the mother's role a bit stereotyped. Do people really say things like that?'

'The last stanza drags on a bit – have you thought about just ending it on the tenth line? I think that would make it stronger, and it's certainly snappier.'

'I didn't understand the plot – why can't the space pilot just go home if the mission doesn't work? Maybe you need to explain that.'

'The rhythm doesn't quite work in line three. Haven't you got one syllable too many there? If you took out darkness and just used dark or night instead it would work.'

As some of these examples illustrate, it can be helpful to phrase comments as questions. These questions are best reflected on later – the workshop is better used to sample readers' impressions than to debate them on the spot, which can use up most of the workshop time. One excellent way of focusing attention purely on the work is to submit all writing for discussion anonymously. If you like, you can 'own up' to whose work is whose at the end of the session, but you do not have to.

When gathering criticism on your own work, remember that the workshop itself is only the point of harvest. The exercise becomes useful when you take the comments you receive home and run them through the mill of your own thoughts. At the workshop itself, it is all too easy to be distracted by a single comment – helpful or unhelpful – and to miss other observations. The importance of listening, rather than leaping into the discussion to try to defend your work, cannot be overestimated. It is most useful to understand your reader's response, least useful to try to refute it as though your work were on trial. For this reason, it can be helpful to record the workshop on tape, or to ask someone in the group to keep a note of the gist of what is said.

FINDING A WORKSHOP

Students on creative writing courses generally have access to workshops. If you are a writer on your own, the search for a writers' group may take a while. Before you begin to look, remember: the most important thing is not to find a workshop, but to find the workshop that is right for you. This may not be the one that is nearest to you, or the one that says the 'nicest' things about your writing, or the one which promises to boost your social life. It will be the one where you find people of similar dedication and seriousness to yourself; people who share your need to read as well as to write.

Writers' groups go under many names: creative writing groups, writers' workshops, poetry circles, writing classes. Groups exist for different reasons. Some are collections of friends, some are organized and run by 'professional' writers or paid tutors. Some exist to promote a particular type of writing. Some use writing as therapy. Some are exclusive, asking prospective members to submit work to show they meet a required standard, while others are happy to welcome anyone. Some are mercilessly analytical, while others are reading groups where everyone gets a round of applause for the courage they have shown in just being prepared to come along and read. The only way to know about a writing group is to suck it and see.

Hunting

Find as many local writing groups as you can. Local libraries are the best and easiest source of information, but also try writing magazines, your regional arts board (which will keep a list of affiliated groups), extra-mural departments and noticeboards in local colleges.

Somewhere, there is probably a group that is just right for you; equally, there are others out there which might be a waste of time, or which could even harm your writing in either of the two best ways of ruining a writer – by convincing you of your own brilliance, or by robbing you of your confidence.

Gathering

Try all the groups you can find. Go at least twice to each one. The first group you visit is unlikely to be the best, or the only one for you. Look around. Write your comments on them in your journal, and then look back over them all. The test is not, did it make me feel wonderful? but, did it help me to write better? This may take a few tries. Did you feel your own critical contributions were welcomed or appreciated? Was there a variety of different styles and subjects presented, or did the group seem to be conforming to a narrow idea of what constituted good writing? Was there a relaxed and good-humoured atmosphere? All these things count. A group cannot help you to write better if it makes you feel uncomfortable, unwelcome, patronized or under-valued. Equally, it cannot help you as a writer if it sends you away every week with a warm glow of recognition of your own genius. If no one present can suggest any worthwhile improvements in your writing, then, bluntly, there is no point in going. If you are serious about your writing, then you are already too advanced to waste your time in mutual admiration societies.

The original meaning of the word poet is 'maker' (as in the old Scots 'makar' or poets). Remember the origins of the word 'workshop'. A workshop is a messy place, a noisy one. There may be heat and sparks. Some of the tools may be sharp. Things get done there. A forge works by means of fire. A constructive group will say things that sometimes hurt your ego. It is unavoidable, unless everything you write is already perfect, and if it is, why are you reading this book?

A good group will have a keen interest in reading the latest and the best that has been published nationally. A group that is only interested in its own work is unlikely to be much help.

Looked around and not found one, or interested in something more adventurous, more up your street? You could always start your own.

STARTING A WORKSHOP

Starting your own writers' group may seem daunting, but remember that most workshops began with someone like you. Someone decided that they wanted to share work, to learn from other people. There are a lot of writers out there. If there is nothing in your area that satisfies you, then the chances are that there are other writers who feel the same way. You just have to find them.

Book a room for a regular slot: writers' groups meet everywhere from rooms above pubs to church halls and sports centres. Try to find somewhere congenial to writing: comfortable and quiet. Avoid using members' homes, at least until the group has built up a basis of mutual trust.

Get your publicity out and remember to leave plenty of time between the date when your notice or advert will go to press and the date of the first meeting. Start with the places where you looked yourself – writers' magazines, college noticeboards, the local library. Put a small ad in the local arts newsletter. See if you can get an article in a community paper or advertising freesheet. If there is nothing around for miles, then make sure your publicity will reach nearby communities from which people might be willing to travel. Bookshops are obviously a prime site for a notice – they are, after all, the one lair where your prey is bound to lurk.

If you can afford it, it can help to get attendance started if you offer refreshment – a lunchtime meeting with a few sandwiches and coffee, an evening one with some drinks. Remember that people who may be shy about their writing need an excuse, as well as a reason, to come along.

Do not be despondent if turnout is low initially. All groups take a while to grow and for word to spread. Give it time. Good groups do not grow overnight. Equally, do not be disillusioned when of the 12 people who turned up for the first two sessions, only half are left for the third.

The group is sorting itself out. Those who are attracted by what you are trying to do and who are prepared to commit time and energy will stay. Those who want easy applause will move on. In time, the group will grow.

TRUST AND CONFIDENCE

Every group works differently. There are no hard and fast rules. You will probably find your group works better, however, if rather than diving straight into passing round members' writing and opening the floor to any kind of comment, you work through a few preparatory phases. Time is on your side: if the group succeeds, it may last for years – many do. The first thing you need to do is to establish trust. To share your writing is a special kind of confiding and difficult to do with strangers. Going for a drink or a meal can help to break down barriers, but this may not be practicably possible. Games and exercises can be shortcuts to the sort of shared knowledge of each other that creates trust and security in a group.

Introductions

The first step in getting to know the members of a group is to learn everyone's name. There are a large number of introductory games. For example: each person in turn can say their name and:

- describe one event from the last week that they could write about;
- say what they would do if they won the lottery; or could design their own perfect day;
- describe the view from their favourite window;
- talk about one object they have owned for a long time;
- talk about the book they would like to write;
- name their three favourite words;
- tell the group what their name means and how they feel about it;
- say three things about themselves, two of which are true and one is false, and ask the others to guess which is true, e.g. *My name's Suzie, I'm a Pisces, I once spent six hours trapped in a telephone box and I have a twin sister.*

All these can initially be done in pairs if the group is large, or one by one if there are fewer people. A variation is for each person to then introduce their pair-partner, and their reply, to the group.

Generating writing

Some groups do this in group time, some do not. For those who find it hard to find time to write, or are short of inspiration, the pressure to produce something and read it out in a limited time can be helpful. While the following exercises refer to poetry, they can easily be adapted to prose or drama.

Take a short poem such as 'Poem to my Wife' by Theodore Roethke. Blank out the key words, photocopy the amended text and let each person fill in the gaps. Read the finished versions to each other, and then read the original text.

Write a poem that meets one of the following criteria: about a stone; with an x or a z in it; to be recited in the dark; to be whispered; that begins with a question; that begins with an exclamation; that begins with its last line and is written backwards; an animal acrostic; that is in someone else's voice.

A regular sequence of workshops featuring writing 'on the spot', readings of short pieces of published work, and reading and discussion of your own work, is the pattern for many groups. Remember that a good workshop takes time to build and that the first weeks are always the hardest. As you get into a routine you should find the process steadily becomes easier and more productive.

Groups can motivate you to produce work which might be hard to do on your own. It can be useful to set each other challenges that are difficult but manageable. For example, write a sonnet in a week.

New departures

Search arts newsletters and the writing press for news of local events. Go to a reading, or a theatre performance, as a group. You could choose a local event, or travel together to a 'big name' event or literary festival some distance away – travel costs can be greatly reduced if, for example, you are able to share a car, or hire a minibus between you.

Magazine prospecting

Ask everyone to choose a different literary magazine, buy one issue and report to the group on what is in it and what they think of it. Afterwards, they can swap them around, or start to create a mini-library.

Competition

Select a poetry or short story competition. Research the judges and their work. Enter as many pieces of work from the group as you can. Read the judges' comments together when they come out with the results. Keep a sense of balance and of humour. Judges are as fallible as any other reader and competition judgements only offer another opinion.

Further projects

Do not feel you have to go to writers – bring them to you. If 20 people can each contribute a few pounds, then together you have a sizeable sum, a fee for which many writers might be happy to come and give a reading, or lead a workshop. There are other sources of finance. Every local authority has a budget for arts development. Regional arts bodies also give grants, as does the lottery. Small sums – a few hundred pounds – are often available, provided that you are prepared to spend the time drafting a convincing application. Generally the events you arrange with such funds must be open to the public, which in turn may help to attract new writers to your group. Choose a writer you find inspirational and challenging and, ideally, who lives fairly near. Writers like to be invited to read. If you can offer a reasonable fee, a bed for the night plus a meal, they may be happy to come to your workshop.

A public reading

Arrange a public performance of your work. It can often be easiest to arrange your reading as part of a larger programme of events, such as a village festival, fair or arts week. Local libraries can be helpful in arranging such events and can sometimes offer a venue. Make sure you get plenty of publicity, remember to rehearse your performance and choose pieces that will go down well with a live audience. Humour is at a premium, as are any works that deal with love, sex and daily life in a lighthearted way. Long, obscure and philosophical works are best left on the page.

Getting away

Residential writing courses such as those run by the Arvon Foundation and the Taliesin Trust in Wales have been turning points in the early writing lives of many authors who are now famous. On the other hand, such courses do not come cheap. Why not organize one your-self?

Some of the essential elements of 'official' writing courses – devoting time only for writing and reading, and immersing yourself in an unfamiliar but inspiring landscape – can be arranged at your own convenience. Off-season accommodation can be surprisingly cheap. If you have built up a relationship with a professional writer, why not ask her to join you and lead a workshop?

CONCLUSION

Never confuse the means – regular contact with a group of writers – with the end: the improvement of your style. In the course of a writer's life there may be associations with several writing groups. You, or other group members, may outgrow a particular workshop and seek a more demanding forum. This is the natural process of creative growth. Approach any workshop in a spirit of sincere and open criticism and support, and the time you spend there will benefit all who attend it.

4 READING AS A WRITER

James Friel

'I read in order to find out what I know: to illuminate the riddle.'
Cynthia Ozick[1]

INTRODUCTION

Reading is the best source of inspiration, the best means to educate yourself, to witness the skill of others – and to witness their disasters. It is through reading you learn to structure a tale, describe character, delineate action, judge what works and what, for you, does not.

How you write, observed the novelist John Gardner,[2] is always an expression – a consequence – of what you have learned from reading. When you write, you are involving yourself in an enormous conversation with everyone else who has done likewise: you learn from them, correct in your own work what you dislike in the work of others, pay tribute to work you admire, establish yourself in a tradition.

There is always something else to read, always some author to discover, another genre to explore. One need not make a distinction between highbrow and lowbrow, good and bad, or divide poetry from prose, screenplay from stage play. Reading is writing's mongrel muse.

Graham Greene's thoughtfully made suspense novels owe as much to the thriller writing skills he learned from reading John Buchan as to the psychologically and structurally more elaborate fictions of Henry James. Samuel Beckett's doleful plays are partly inspired by the great clowns of stage and screen, and Woody Allen's comedies arise from a love of the far gloomier films of Ingmar Bergman. More recently, a film like Curtis Hanson's *LA Confidential* (1998) pays homage to Roman Polanski's *Chinatown* (1976) which, in turn, borrows its look and sound from *films noirs* of the late 1940s, such as Howard Hawks' version of *The Big Sleep* (1948). James Elroy's novel, *LA Confidential* owes much to the work of Raymond Chandler, author of *The Big Sleep*, and Chandler comes out of a tradition of pulp writing in the 1920s and 30s. Pulp fiction may be termed lowbrow, but Chandler's work is also heavily influenced by the work of Thomas Malory and the legends of King Arthur.

Films, poems, stories, plays, song lyrics – whatever you read, have read, will read – will filter into your own writing. Reading – like everything else but much more so – is grist to a writer's mill. How your reading informs your writing is a complex process and worth investigating.

Be a replicant

The novelist, children's writer and film-maker, Philip Ridley, once made a list of 100 texts – comics, films, novels, songs, poems – explaining, 'If you were to make a replicant of me (à la *Blade Runner*) these should be the first things filed in my memory.'[3]

Start with the first text that comes into your mind. Make a note of the possible reasons why that one surfaces before all others, and then go on to do the same for a second or a third text. If it helps, let them emerge in a chain of associations: books you read as a child; books you read now; books you loathed; books you read as a guilty pleasure; books you have never read but feel as if you had; a poem you memorized when you were nine; a film that has invaded your dreams ever since you first saw it; a song that summons the past. Keep going. Work at this for half an hour, allowing film to follow book follow comic follow poem follow play follow pop song. Do not discriminate. See what comes. This is a map of your reading life, its suburbs, its palaces, its canals, its back streets and motorways.

Consider what you have done. What are the common features in your list? What obsessions does it reveal, what themes and interests?

Think of the things you have written, are writing and most wish to write. Do they tally? How? If not, why not? Are you writing something you would not read? Is that wise? Are you writing exactly what you wish to read? What is that exactly?

The questions, once they start, are endless. Let them keep coming. They should occupy you all your writing life.

INFLUENCES

But what about originality? What about your essential vision? What about being – intake of breath – 'influenced'?

'Influenced' by the best minds, the best styles, the most effective artists our civilization has known? To be influenced by Proust? Perverted from true originality by the siren call of George Eliot? To read your contemporaries and find out what they are doing and you are not? Oh how terrible the damage will be.

That said, certain writers can get into your bones. Iris Murdoch said she could not write a novel and read Henry James. She caught his style like measles. And some writers – the great stylists – can be infectious in this way.

This is not an argument against reading; it is an argument for reading more.

Change the words but keep the syntax

Take any opening paragraph of a writer you either particularly admire or a writer of whom you fear you are too fond and liable to be 'influenced' by – whose voice may drown yours out, perhaps. Take Jane Austen's *Emma*:

> Emma Woodhouse, handsome, clever, and rich, with a comfortable home and a happy disposition, seemed to unite some of the best blessings of existence; and had lived nearly twenty-one years in the world with very little to distress or vex her.

Now change the words but keep the syntax. Stick to the same number of syllables and – if you can hear them – the same rhythms and stresses in the prose.

> Janet Worswick, pretty, witty and wise, with an exuberant heart and healthy constitution, loved to wrestle some of the best wrestlers in Llangollen; and had fought nearly forty-two men with hardly any to exhaust or defeat her.

Austen may win hands down, but in the struggle you will have learned how balanced that syntax is, how rhythmic and precise, how freighted with irony. Isn't this useful knowledge? And you have a short piece of original writing that might go somewhere – who knows?[4]

Try something similar with a writer you admire or whose influence you wish to exorcize.

You will only be influenced in a negative way if you read without understanding. Many writers avoid reading while involved in writing, but this is wise only if writing all-out or in short bursts. If your work takes years to complete, are you really going to stop reading throughout that period – when you most need to investigate what it has to offer?

Take a leaf out of Flannery O'Connor's book and read good prose before you start a day's writing. Annie Dillard warms up by reading pure sound unencumbered by sense – Conrad Aiken's poetry, or 'any poetry anthology's index of first lines'. Reading immediately before you write is what some writers call 'priming the pump'. If what you read stains your own work, what harm? Work through it. Isn't this one of the reasons you redraft?

Never fight shy of letting your writing come out of your reading. There has always been a relationship between the two. Virgil modelled *The Aeneid* on Homer's epic poems and Milton's *Paradise Lost* is an attempt to equal in English what was done by them in Latin and in Greek. Fielding's *Tom Jones* is both a homage to and a satire of the classical epic and James Joyce's *Ulysses* uses *The Odyssey* for its very bones.

Writing comes out of reading either directly – Susan Hill writing a sequel to *Rebecca*, Leon Garfield completing Dickens's *Edwin Drood* – or sideways, as Jean Rhys's oblique recreation of *Jane Eyre* in *Wide Sargasso Sea* or Peter Carey's re-appraisal of *Great Expectations* in *Jack Maggs*, or Kathy Acker's cut-and-come-again version of the same novel. Donald Barthelme rewrites 'Snow White', Coetzee rewrites 'the true tale of Robinson Crusoe' in *Foe*. Borrowings may be more deceptive, as in Angela Carter's comic reworking of all Shakespeare's plays in the plot of *Wise Children*, and Richard Beard's novel *Damascus*, where the author uses only those words used in a single issue of *The Times*.

Suggestions for writing

Relying on the spine of a classic tale or dreaming up the back story of an established text can provide help and inspiration to write. Take a story which you know well – one that fascinates you (from the list you made in the 'replicant' exercise, perhaps) – and write a plan or synopsis in which you:

- change the point of view
- change the location
- change the period.

Re-read a novel or story that you already know well, with the specific intention of taking note of either:

- clothing
- colour
- the weather.

Underline any reference to one of these subjects and notice how seemingly inconsequential details often added primarily to make a convincing background can also carry plot points and be an implicit means of developing character. See how a writer can use weather, building up heat so that the storm with which the tale ends is a natural culmination of details that had appeared incidental, or how, in Henry James's *Washington Square*, a woman who wears gaudy red gowns lightens her wardrobe as the story goes on until in the last chapter she is in bridal white – but we know that she will end her life a spinster. Such details work best at a subliminal level. Sharpen your eyes and ears as a reader. Nabokov in his *Lectures on Literature*[5] would have you draw Anna Karenina's hair from Tolstoy's description, or the carriage ridden in by Emma and Leon in Flaubert's *Madame Bovary* – so sensuous an activity is reading, so magical a process is writing.

Find the screenplay of a film and either imagine or storyboard two or three scenes before watching it, deciding where you would place the camera and use music and how you would instruct the actors. Compare your ideas with the finished product.

Take the first page of an existing novel – or even a sample of your own prose – and adapt it for either stage or screen. For prose writers, this can be an effective editing exercise, cutting a scene down to its essentials. You can, of course, do the reverse: take a script and novelize it.

Take a book from your shelves that you have yet to read. After studying the blurb, the reviews or anything else on its cover, write what you imagine might be the opening paragraph and then compare your own attempt with the actual opening. This is an excellent way of kick-starting a piece of writing and investigating another writer's technique – and your own. It is particularly useful when considering genre fiction such as crime or sci-fi. Your own version may be different – better even. If so, you are free to continue with it.

A not dissimilar exercise is inspired by Raymond Queneau's *Exercise in Style*,[6] a collection of 99 short pieces that recount the same banal incident in different styles. The narrator bumps into a long-necked man on a bus and later sees him in a train station in the company of a friend who fixes a button on his coat. Before you read this fascinating, witty book, recount the above incident as a chapter in a romantic novel, a spy story, a detective story, a western, a Greek tragedy.

Will this more self-conscious way of reading take the pleasure out of a favoured leisure pursuit? Initially, yes, but what is gained is knowledge, insight, confidence, ideas and inspiration. Reading for a writer is a form of work, another way of thinking about writing. A writer is always hunting, looking to snatch or steal, discovering what to avoid and what to make your own.

The practice of poetry

In his last collection of poetry,[7] Raymond Carver began to write out passages from Chekhov's stories, turning the prose into poetry simply by using line breaks. A. S. Byatt in her novel, *Possession*, takes a passage from James's *The Golden Bowl* and, with a little tampering, turns it into poetry 'written' by her hero, a fictional Victorian poet. This is a useful habit for both poets and prose writers. Practising poetry can teach prose writers a great deal about the heft of individual words, about placing them in a sentence to gain effect, poise, spin. Simply write out the prose and insert a line break where you would naturally want or insist upon a pause if it were being spoken aloud.

Prose writers learn from poets. As John Gardner puts it: 'Prose, like poetry, is built of rhythms and rhythmic variations ... Rhythm and variation are as basic to prose as to poetry. All prose must force rhythms, just like verse.'[8] Take one of your own sentences and follow Gardner's example. Read or read again Chapter 8, 'Writing poetry'.

In order to do the above exercises you will have had to read your work aloud – or at least mumble it. Do not fight shy of doing this. It is a way of making your words other, hearing them outside yourself. If you write for children, for instance, how else are you going to learn what pleases them and keeps their attention? Learning what captivates an audience is not so dissimilar to learning what captivates the individual reader. May Sarton considered a reading of a poem to an audience as similar to making a final draft.[9]

People say that the internet is putting an end to reading. How can this be when the internet is almost nothing but text and a great store of knowledge? And as Annie Proulx advises, think of all the things a writer needs to know: 'I need to know which mushrooms smell like maraschino cherries and which like dead rats ... [and] that a magpie in flight briefly resembles a wooden spoon ...'[10]

You can apply the same system of grazing the net as you do a bookshelf or encyclopaedia or dictionary. Graze. The rules of surfing – like those of what Annie Proulx calls road drift – are simple: always take a branching side route, stop often, get out and listen, walk around, see what you see.

DO AS YOU WOULD BE DONE BY

The writer Nathaniel Bentley said he found bookshops too depressing to enter. All those books – each an attempt at immortality – mouldering on the shelves unread, unloved.

You must read them. You must love them. Who else will keep the art of reading alive if not writers? Rescue the past. Find out your own unloved books and writers. Adopt them. Rediscover the best of those we have left behind and out of print. One day your book might be among them, waiting for a future reader, a future writer to hunt it out.

CONCLUSION

Read the world as if it were a text. Consume it and find words to convey your experiences; then weave them into stories. This is what a writer does: turns the world into text so that there is ever more to read, ever more to write.

Notes

1 Cynthia Ozick, *Writers at Work: The Paris Review Interviews*, eighth series (Viking Penguin, New York, 1988).
2 John Gardner, *The Art of Fiction* (Alfred A. Knopf, New York, 1984).
3 Philip Ridley in *The Test of Time: What Makes a Classic a Classic*, ed. by Andrew Holgate and Honor Wilson-Fletcher (Waterstones Magazine Publication, London, 1999).
4 This exercise is borrowed from Dorothea Brande's *Becoming a Writer* (Macmillan, London, 1983).
5 Vladimir Nabokov, *Lectures on Literature* (Harcourt Brace Jovanovich, New York and London, 1980).
6 Raymond Queneau, *Exercise in Style* (Marion Boyars, London, 1972).
7 Raymond Carver, *The Path to the Waterfall* (Harvill Collins, New York, 1989).
8 Gardner, *The Art of Fiction*.
9 May Sarton, *Journal of a Solitude* (Women's Press, London, 1985).
10 Annie Proulx, New York Times News Service, 1999.

5 WORKING WITH MYTH

Edmund Cusick

INTRODUCTION

Myths are the first stories. The age of myths is measured not in years but in thousands of years. Within myths are experiences and intuitions so powerful that they grow within a culture as time passes, told and retold down the generations. Myths are stories which encode intuitions of the way the world is. Every culture has myths to explain our beginnings: the Yoruba myth of the first men coming to earth on a ladder spun by a spider, the Indian story of Yama and Yami, the first man and woman, or the Hebrew story of the Garden of Eden.

Why use myths? Why breathe oxygen? We have no choice. To tell stories is as natural to us as breathing. We are, in a sense, made of stories: every culture in every age has told stories and these stories form our understanding of ourselves and the world. We may have swapped the campfire for the soap opera, tales of marvels for gossip and urban legends, but our hunger for stories remains as keen as ever. Even soap opera plots develop mythic dimensions at times: the body under the patio, the secret act of incest can, for a week or a month, grip the collective imagination.

Compulsive stories

In your journal write down, in note form, any story you have heard in the last fortnight. Try to think of one which you felt you had to tell to someone else (it could be, for example, a film plot, a joke, a twist in a TV serial, or an anecdote about someone you know). What is its appeal – surprise, humour, shock? Jot down other stories you have told more than once: particularly any you may have retold over several years. What was their appeal?

As individuals, we arrange the way we understand ourselves, our own lives and those whose lives have touched ours, into stories: in our letters, our conversations and our diaries. At a deeper level still, we weave stories in our own heads, sometimes without realizing it: personal myths of where we have come from, of what we may achieve, of the fateful events that have led to our greatest triumphs or disasters. We live within these stories, shaping our sense of our lives, continually composing and recomposing. To be aware of this is one step towards fiction writing.

Before writers there were tellers. All literature has its roots in oral tradition. In storytelling, there is a tradition known as 'the ladder to the stars'. The best illustration of this is a whole night given over to story-telling, during which there is a natural progression from personal anecdote to tales of the family and ancestors, from tales of the ancestors to heroes, from tales of heroes to the deeds of the gods and the great story of the creation of the world. Even for those who have no interest in oral storytelling, the personal can serve as a gateway to understanding and writing myth. The key to working with myth is being able to find a point of imaginative contact where the universal can, for you, become personal.

Deceit

Tell a lie about yourself to someone else. About your history, your family, your life experience. Introduce yourself by a false name; invent an imaginary sister; hint of your time in the Foreign Legion. But let the name, the life story, the scandalous cousin, be something you wish were true, or that you feel should be true: something that is true on the inside, if not on the outside. Go on. Try it. You can always confess later: then again, you might decide not to.

Life history

Write the story of your life, in exactly 100 words. Each of the words must only be one syllable. It is tempting to cheat a bit, but follow these rules exactly. Read your story back to yourself. It is your own life, stripped down to essentials. It can be surprising how a deep narrative, an underlying pattern, comes through.

Find out as much as you can about your family's history, for as many generations as you can trace. Do you have family legends about characters living or dead? If so, what do they say about you as a family and why do you think those stories have been passed down?

Roots

In your writer's journal, summarize the most significant movements and events in your family's history, and note any narratives within it – perhaps of a distant relative – which grip your imagination. How do you feel about this inheritance? Is it one you identify with, or one you wish to pull away from? Can you think of a story that sums up your attitude to life, for example, or a story of one thing you have done that you would like your descendants to tell about you? If so, record it.

Memory

Write in note form any myth or legend you remember, if only roughly. Why does it stick in your mind? Try to remember where you first heard the myth and any other sources in which you have come across different versions. Note anything that intrigued you, or left you puzzled or unsatisfied. If you had to repeat the myth to someone else, how would you expand on these points to make sense of them?

Myth and the self

Choose any myth or legend you remember and write it as a story of three or four pages. Begin it with the word 'I' and make the second word the name of its heroine or hero. Take the central character and become them imaginatively, so that the whole story is told in the first person.

FINDING MYTHS

Books of myths and legends from a range of traditions are widely available: one fine example is Kevin Crossley Holland's *The Norse Myths*. Note that traditional stories are often designed to be told orally: this means that, when written down, they appear in skeletal form, no more than summaries of the action and some lines of dialogue. *The Mabinogion* and Robert Graves' *The Greek Myths* are both examples. Do not be disappointed by this. The gaps are there for you, the teller or the writer, to fill from your own imagination, and the story's skeleton contains all that you will need to bring it to life in your own way.

Read a sample of myths from different cultures: Indian, Irish, Greek, Welsh, Egyptian. You will find that some seem more in tune with your imagination than others. If there is a place which figures in your own story, or your family's, start there. If you have links with India, for example, you could begin with the *Ramayana*. Browse through your books until you find an appealing character or incident. Some bodies of mythology have less to do with a nation than with a religion. The Bible, for example, is one of our most influential sources of mythology. Read it in the authorized or King James translation. Begin with the book of Genesis, with its stories of the creation of the world, the supernatural encounters between the sons of God and the daughters of men, Cain and Abel, and Jacob wrestling with an angel.

Cinema and myth

See Chapter 7 on writing for screen and television and on the archetypal patterns which can work in film plots. There are countless examples of myth influencing recent films. Look at *Blade Runner*, *Devil's Advocate*, *The Warriors*, *The Blue Lagoon*, *Raiders of the Lost Ark* and *Splash*. The more you read in myth, the more you will recognize mythic elements in the plots of films.

Heroes

Almost all myths have a hero, male or female. Typically, tales of epics feature in the hero's birth and upbringing, while in their marvellous deeds (often involving a quest for some precious goal, which may take years to fulfil) the hero generates action, creating further stories. From Jason and the Argonauts to Frodo and Aragorn (Tolkien was himself a professor of heroic Anglo-Saxon literature) to *Star Wars*, *The X-Files*, *Xena: Warrior Princess* and Lara Croft, the hero is one of the most magnetic figures in fiction. The genre of fantasy, from books to computer games, abounds with heroes, as do most other varieties of genre fiction, from thrillers to detective stories. To create a hero is one of the most liberating and enjoyable forms of imaginative invention.

Birth of a hero

Invent your own hero, writing notes on his or her origins, gifts, mission, friends and principal opponents. Have fun. If you can both enjoy your hero and take her seriously, the chances are that your reader will do both also. Remember that not all heroes are entirely likeable – many have one or more vices, which complicate their nature and the reader's reactions.

The following exercises are based on heroic narratives of Greek myths but can, of course, be adapted to suit your own favourite material.

Entering the myth: heroes and victims

Find the story of the labyrinth and the Minotaur in Robert Graves' *The Greek Myths*. Read the whole story from its beginnings with Poseidon, Pasiphae and the bull. Imaginatively enter the story as Ariadne, or as Theseus. Choose one moment from the story and write their thoughts. Then choose another character at that same moment: King Minos, Daedalus, Pasiphae – the Minotaur itself.

Transforming the myth

Think of ways in which you could use the story to work with themes, characters or landscapes of your own. What would the labyrinth be in your dreamscape, the landscape of your own imagination? An underground rail network, a maze in a country house, a tormented soul with a complex and bewildering psyche, an alien spaceship, a huge corporation where no one trusts anybody else? Who would you have explore such a place and what is the most shocking monster that might be trapped there? Use this as a starting point for a poem, screenplay or story. Though you do not have to follow the original story in every detail, returning to the myth will often offer positive inspiration as to how to progress.

Myth, legend and landscape

The land we live in is inhabited by stories. This is reflected in the many sites which bear Arthur's name or are otherwise associated with Arthurian myth. The myth of King Arthur has survived from the Celtic dark ages to the present day, passing from story to painting to poem to novel and film. Both the Arthurian paradise of Avalon and the Celtic underworld Annwn were believed to have a hidden location somewhere around the islands of Britain. Many other sites are associated with ancient legends: the Grand Canyon, Iona, the Giant's Causeway, Stonehenge, Glastonbury, Sherwood Forest, the Ganges, Tintagel, Loch Ness and the Blue Mosque in Istanbul all bear their histories. There will be legendary places near you – haunted tower blocks, black dogs, buried treasure, spots you must avoid at all costs at midnight. Find them out. It may help to read books such as Janet and Colin Bord's *Atlas of Magical Britain*[1] and Ean Begg's *On the Trail of Merlin*.[2] Use your holiday travels to collect more stories – another way of getting to know a place. This can prove rewarding whether you travel in Britain or abroad. Crete, for example, is the site of the labyrinth, Rome has its legends – and tourist souvenirs – of Romulus and Remus suckled by a she-wolf, and the dragon on the Welsh flag belongs to one of the oldest stories of Britain.

Local legend

Find a local site famous for a legend or folk tale: for example, Wayland's Smithy in Oxfordshire. You can learn more about the story of Wayland in Geoffrey Ashe's *Mythologies of the British Isles*.[3] Read it at the site, or go in a group and let one person tell the legend to the others. If you do go in a group, try not to talk about your own creative ideas until you return. Jealously guard your own inspiration.

MYTH AND SYMBOL

Myth is more than a body of stories – it opens into a way of thought associated with inner, intuitive order rather than the cold logic of fact. Myth is intimately linked to both the creative imagination and the unconscious.

Myth, though often transcribed in prose, resembles those works of poetry which are driven not by the necessity to obey outer realism – the world as we see it – but rather the compulsions and fears of the world behind our eyes. The narrative can seem at times no more than a structure to contain images – grotesque, arresting, beautiful – which have been thrown up from our desires or dreams. Two obvious examples are images of magical transformation, and the many strange combinations of human and animal which run through most mythic traditions. Such myths can offer a gateway into the worlds of symbol – a shape borrowed from the outer world but charged with inner meaning – and of magic: the ability to abandon the laws of causality for the reign of supernatural order. The story of Blodeuwedd, in the fourth branch of *The Mabinogion*, is an illustration of a tale driven by magical symbolism: its heroine is transformed from flower to woman to owl, and her spouse, in the moment of death, becomes an eagle, and is then charmed into human form once more.

The exercises that follow are rather different from those elsewhere in the book – they are exercises in imagination, rather than in writing *per se*. They may seem strange, tiring, or to use an older word, weird. Try them anyway, particularly when you can be relaxed and undisturbed.

The shape changer

Choose a time when you can relax completely. You may find that the moments of going to sleep or waking are the best. Imagine yourself as an animal – any animal – a leopard, an eagle, a cat. Move through your five senses as you would in animal form. Discover the joys of swimming, flying, crawling, hunting.

Dreams

Gather material from a dream diary (See Chapter 2). Look out in particular for elements that do not stem directly from your daily life. See if the stories of your dreams exemplify your personal myths. You may find Jung's book, *Man and his Symbols*, useful.[4]

The inner room

Systematically construct your perfect place. It might be a palace, a beach, a church or temple, a hillside or wood. You can start from a place which you know, but feel free to adapt it as you rebuild it in your mind. You cannot do this at one go. Return to it, perhaps daily or nightly, enjoying the peace or exhilaration it offers. After a while it will develop its own energy, its own certainty, and you will not need to put effort into constructing it. Discover new things in it. Design a gate or doorway which you open and close behind you as you enter or leave it. Take time to create this doorway, so that it, too, reflects your character and tastes.

CONCLUSION

You will see how Chapters 7 and 11 refer to basic story patterns, and how Chapter 9 refers to fairy tale, another branch of traditional story. These models have not been chosen by chance. Myths are at the core of literature. You cannot go far without beginning to rub shoulders with myth, though it is possible to do so without knowing it. Many of the greatest works of art make contact with myth. Try looking at John Burnside's *Swimming in the Flood*,[5] Seamus Heaney's *Beowulf*,[6] James Joyce's *Portrait of the Artist as a Young Man*,[7] Ted Hughes' *Birthday Letters*.[8] Read the work of Charlotte Brontë, Vicki Feaver, Hilary Llewellyn-Williams, Rose Flint and Michèle Roberts.

If you try too hard to evoke such symbolic echoes, they will elude you, or seem forced. But if you open your imagination to myth, your writing will sound its resonances to your readers.

Notes

1 Janet and Colin Bord, *Atlas of Magical Britain* (Sidgwick and Jackson, London, 1990).
2 Deike Rich and Ean Begg, *On the Trail of Merlin: A Guide to the Celtic Mystery Tradition* (Aquarian Press, London, 1991).
3 Geoffrey Ashe, *Mythologies of the British Isles* (Guild, London, 1991).

4 C. G. Jung (ed.), *Man and his Symbols* (Picador, London, 1999).
5 John Burnside, *Swimming in the Flood* (Cape, London, 1999).
6 Seamus Heaney (trans.), *Beowulf* (Faber and Faber, London, 1999).
7 James Joyce, *Portrait of the Artist as a Young Man* (Penguin, Harmondsworth, 1999).
8 Ted Hughes, *Birthday Letters* (Faber and Faber, London, 1999).

Part Two: Advancing

6 SHORT STORY WRITING

Jenny Newman

INTRODUCTION

The short story is the best place to start writing fiction. It can be long enough to let you build character, write dialogue, experiment with different plots, and in general flex your writing muscles; but it need not be so long that you get bogged down, or lose your sense of direction. Because of its brevity and precision, the short story gives you invaluable training in the skill of editing. You may, if you wish, redraft it from start to finish, polish it, and bring all your talents to bear on it, and not lose touch with your initial impulse. As V. S. Pritchett says, 'The novel tends to tell us everything, whereas the short story tells us only one thing, and that intensely.'[1]

Though the short story's roots are in the fairy tales, moral fables, folk tales and ghost stories our ancestors told round the fire, its descendants are just as at home in the age of sudden fiction and the soundbite. People's first response to a life crisis is often to reshape it as a story, for themselves or somebody else. It is the art of the present moment, a snapshot rather than a biography. The short story writer does not need to spell out what happened before, or what will happen next. Instead, she learns to select those images and details which will resonate in the mind of her reader or listener, and make him feel he knows all he needs to know about characters and setting.

The short story writer depends on what Raymond Carver calls 'a unique and exact way of looking at things, and [on] finding the right context for expressing that way of looking'.[2] This is the ideal form in which to begin uncovering your writer's 'voice', that singular slant on experience and way of describing it that will distinguish your work from everyone else's.

BEGINNING

The blank page is often daunting, and the best advice is to start your story anywhere you can. See Chapter 2, 'Keeping a writer's journal', on how to make sure that you do not waste precious writing time struggling to dredge up ideas. Your inspiration may be an overheard snippet of conversation, an image hoarded against a rainy day, or the pulse of an idea which lodges itself in your imagination and insists that you elaborate on it. Whatever your starting point, commit it to paper as soon as you can.

Any first paragraph which engages your reader is a success. Any other is a failure. If your beginning seems inert, remember that the shadow of a future conflict is a sure way to spark interest. Enter the first scene as late as you can without being baffling, and plant a 'hook' or attention grabber as soon as possible. This could be a question, implicit or explicit, to be answered by the rest of the story.

Let us take, for example, these four opening lines of dialogue:

'Nice day,' said Katy, lacing her trainers.
Amira banged the kettle on to the hob. 'What's so nice about it?'
Katy's face was bright with laughter. 'Aren't you going to tell me what's up?'
'I don't want to talk about it,' said Amira. 'Let's just get it over with.'

We know early on that Amira is upset about something. When Katy tackles her about her mood, she refuses to communicate. This should ring alarm bells in the reader's head. *What is the problem that Amira does not wish to discuss?* Then Amira adds 'Let's just get it over with.' The pronoun 'it' appears twice on the same line. Does it refer to two different problems, or to the same one? With any luck your reader is already hooked. Now help her picture the setting with some 'weather in the streets'; but do not load her with information too early on, or insert long flashbacks which distract her from the narrative present.

Take the time to choose a good title, because it is what may strike your reader first. There are many possible approaches. Your title may, for instance, be the name of the central character, or of an object of significance to the plot. It can be long enough to tell part of the story, or consist of only one word; or else it can be a key to reading the story itself, as in Michael Carson's 'All over the place'.[3]

CHARACTER

Frank O'Connor believes that the short story is the province of what he calls 'submerged population groups' such as 'tramps, artists, lonely idealists, dreamers and spoilt priests'.[4] Even if you do not know any such people, keep an eye open for those who live at odds with the so-called mainstream. Adapted to the demands of your plot, their imagined insights may well fuel a story. Traditional tales often describe a magical or out-of-the-way episode, and many modern short story writers treasure this link with what is odd, uncanny or bizarre. Writing from a new, divergent perspective is part of what the French novelist Albert Camus called 'defamiliarization', or making the ordinary look strange, and it can be seen as the short story's – as opposed to the novel's – distinguishing characteristic.

Modern readers can grow bored with description, so introduce your story people economically and memorably. It is more entertaining to reveal a character through the way he or she drives, smokes, or reads the paper than by resorting to tired descriptions of hair and eye colour. Dialogue, action, dress and physiognomy can all be pressed into service. Learn to name names. If you write, 'Melvyn hopped into his shiny red Porsche', your reader will learn more than if you write, 'Melvyn got into his car'. Though it may take some research, consider inventing a main character who is different from you in, say, age, class, experience or gender. For advice on people watching, and gathering raw material for your stories, read Chapter 1 on 'Observation and discovery'. Choosing an unfamiliar character may help you to find a voice which differs from your everyday tone, and thus make your writing more distinctive.

Your main character can be central to the action, or else confined to the sidelines. There are many successful examples of overlooked or impotent central characters, such as the paralysed man in Rose Tremain's 'My Wife is a White Russian'[5] being bullied by his wife in an expensive restaurant, but it may be easier to start with one who initiates the action.

As the resolution will depend on a change taking place, choose a main character who is capable of a realization or transformation which, however small, can be shown to be crucial. Intimate at least the shadow of that change by the end of your first page.

Make your main character memorable

Write a short paragraph describing your main character. Even if it does not all find its way into the finished story, it will belong to the 90 per cent of the iceberg which you alone know, and not the 10 per cent seen by the reader. It is this 'underwater' knowledge which lends conviction to the details you select. When describing a character's appearance, do not linger on what is predictable, but find a feature which sticks out from the norm, or hints at a hidden trait, or spells insight or disaster. 'Celia Jones had a face like the blade of an axe.' What does this mean for the plot? How does it point to the end of your story?

Your reader will take at most half an hour to read or listen to your short story, and usually less, so keep your cast to a maximum (excluding walk-on roles) of three or four.

POINT OF VIEW

Point of view is a literary term for the lens through which your reader looks at the world of your story.

Your basic choice is between choosing a *character-narrator* and *writing in the third person*. (Technically, if you choose the latter, you will be writing as an author-narrator, not a character-narrator.)

Character-narrator

If one of your characters is telling the story, you are committed to writing in either (a) the first person or, very unusually, (b) the second person.

First-person character-narrator

> My mother says I take after my dad, not her. I was a scally at school, sagging regularly, and bent on leaving as soon as I could to earn the money to buy myself a good time – a good time being pubbing and clubbing.[6]

This is a standard choice, and particularly good for beginners, because handled well it locates your reader firmly in the mind of one character. Many famous writers continue to exploit this voice because of what Graham Swift calls the located, ground-level view it gives. Its success depends on your ability to find a convincing voice and stick to it, cutting any authorial flourishes which take us outside your character-narrator's head.

Despite its popularity, this method has some drawbacks. It is obviously difficult to end with the death of a first-person narrator. Also, it is a difficult mode in which to tell your reader more than your character-narrator might reasonably know, and this can be uncomfortably limiting if, say, your narrator is a child, which may be why many short stories about young children are written in the third person. More crucially, it is hard to describe your narrator's appearance, or any important change of expression, or anything else that she cannot see for herself. But there are ways of overcoming this handicap. Another character may comment on your narrator's looks; or else you can resort to the traditional method of having her look in the mirror.

Second-person character-narrator

> You unzipped your dress without closing the curtains, and kicked it to the floor. Wearing only your silk cami-knickers, you flopped on to your divan and took a last swig from the bottle of Chardonnay. Then you passed out with your cigarette burning.

Although its rarity lends freshness, this is a difficult voice through which to structure a story. In Jamaica Kincaid's 'Girl', for instance, the story's introduction, climax and resolution are all created through the rhetoric of the mother-speaker, as is the character of the daughter whom she is haranguing. This challenging form is close to the dramatic monologue, more fully discussed in Chapter 9, 'Writing for stage'.

Third person

Though there are many variants of this mode, your basic choice is between:

(a) limited point of view
(b) omniscience
(c) objectivity.

Third-person *limited* point of view

> He had his theme. But whenever he sat down at his word processor the facility which had once made writing a pleasure – and brought him a brief notoriety – eluded him, evanescing like the smoke from the illicit cigarettes he lit one after another and leaving him with a sour mouth and pulsing head.[7]

Like the first person, this narrative method is popular for its tight focus. It allows you to look through the eyes of your main character, or any other character you believe would make a good vantage point. Again like the first person, its success depends on your finding a convincing and sustainable voice; but it gives you a little more freedom. For example, if you are skilled, it is possible to speak, as it were, over your point-of-view character's head. In James Joyce's 'Clay'[8] the reader, unlike the point-of-view character, Maria, knows that the man on the bus is a thief and (helped by the story's title) that the soft wet substance that Maria touches is garden clay. The title also helps in Graham Greene's 'I Spy',[9] where we know what the 12-year-old Charlie cannot: that his father has been spying for the Germans. This story also demonstrates another advantage of the third-person limited viewpoint: you can draw back far enough to describe how your point-of-view character looks, what he is wearing, or a change in his appearance, without sabotaging your point of view.

Third-person *omniscient* (all-knowing) narrator

This is for the days when you are bent on playing God.

> There is nothing of consequence in a red balloon but the six-year-old heiress, Grace Cooper Glass, marvels at it, open-mouthed, and forgets to even breathe. She is charmed that something so round and fatly red

can fly and Master Milltown Blake is charmed by her. She is so young, so plump, so volatile.

In the lives that are to come, each will remember this moment, slight though it is; the red balloon, Washington Square, the spring day's petal sheen. They will record it, recreate it time and again in letters, diaries, poetry and prose. They will be the most important person in each other's lives. They will anchor one another.[10]

Though still associated with Victorian novelists, this method may be making a comeback. As omniscient narrator you may inhabit the mind of any character you wish, describe their pasts and predict their futures, and interpret their feelings. You may also address the reader directly, or communicate universal truths or matters of principle; but be sparing with your facts and observations, because few modern readers like to be lectured. If you exhort them too much, or they feel you are showing off at their expense, they may grow alienated, and stop reading.

In so short and intense a form it is seldom possible to do all these things; but there are many degrees of omniscience. You may, if you wish, restrict yourself to two or three characters, or nip into one mind only briefly, or throw your reader no more than an occasional comment. Feel free to experiment, and decide which mode suits you best. But remember that, like changing lanes on the motorway, it is dangerous to switch viewpoints at random. Your reader can become confused and unsettled.

Third-person *objective* point of view

The store detective's nose twitched. 'So this cardigan fell into your shopping bag?'

The woman's shoes were down at heel and her calves blotched with chilblains. 'Yes,' she said. 'I think it must have done.'

'That's very likely.' The detective's fish-eyes turned cold. 'Now let's see what the Manager has to say.'

In this mode the narrator stays outside every character's point of view, and confines him or herself to noting about all of them what anyone in their vicinity might observe. The most famous exponent of this form is Ernest Hemingway, who in many of his short stories gives his readers the data necessary to know his characters better than they know themselves. It all depends on the quality of observation. The pleasure of this mode is that it often makes the reader feel astute. The snag is that it can feel a little cold, with so much hinging on the gap between what characters do and what they say, and with their feelings deduced rather than explored.

When you establish a point of view at the start of a story, you implicitly invite the reader to enter into a contract: this is the way that together we will see the world. If that contract is broken through your carelessness or lack of skill, you will risk losing your reader. For any voice to be convincing, you must abide by its limitations, and devise ways where necessary to overcome them.

Childhood memory

Write down a memory from the years before you were 10. It could relate to your first day at school, the arrival of a brother or sister, the death of a pet, the first Christmas you remember: anything you like, no matter how small, as long as it aroused deep feeling in your child-hood self. Write as freely as you can, not letting the nib of your pen leave the page. Try and inhabit the child that you were then, and remember to use all your senses: the smell of a classroom, or a nappy, the sound of a baby's cry, your first close look at Santa Claus, or the feeling of a bird's feathers.

After waiting a day or two, rewrite the episode in the third person from the point of view of someone else involved in the story, such as a parent or schoolmate. They need not have played a major part in your first account. All you have to do is get inside his or her head and stay there, remembering that a shift of point of view can alter the plot (an event which is important to one person may be insignificant to another).

You may, if you wish, experiment with all the points of view outlined above, or try writing in a different tense, then compare your two versions. What are their strengths and weaknesses?

DIALOGUE

Dialogue is a great enlivener. Well handled, it can develop character and propel the plot. It can also vary the narrative pacing, deftly reveal your characters' incomes, jobs, geographical region, and class, and lend texture and atmosphere to your prose style. The first rule of good dialogue is to use it.

The second rule is not to confuse it with everyday speech. Realism is a literary convention – or set of conventions – and its dialogue works harder than everyday talk. Avoid exchanges which in real life would express nothing more than a general sociability (this speech mode is sometimes known as the phatic):

'Oh, hi, Tony, my name's Avril,' said Avril confidently.
'Hello, Avril. Pleased to meet you,' responded Tony.
'Me likewise,' commented Avril.
'What do you think of this weather?' asked Tony.
'Awful. Let's hope it clears for the weekend,' averred Avril.

'Well, I must be going,' replied Tony.
'See you, Tony,' called Avril.

Though exaggeratedly bad, these lines may demonstrate how inept dialogue can ruin a story. Overturning the first rule of dialogue ('use it'), the encounter would have been better summarized as 'one day Avril introduced herself to Tony'. Nor do your characters need to keep calling each other by name – it clutters the prose. Be sparing with adverbs (such as 'loudly') attached to speech tags (such as 'he said'). If you must mention volume, for example, it is better to choose a verb – in this case, 'bellow' might do – which incorporates the adverb's meaning. In general it is better to stick with the almost invisible he said/she said, because a lot of different tags (replied, commented, averred, called, shouted) distracts the reader. The most elegant solution is to dispense with all possible speech tags. As long as you begin a fresh line with each new speaker, and give each character their own speech pattern, you can expect your reader to do some work.

Cut out from your dialogue any information already known to the reader from the narrative. Though dialogue can drive the action, it should never be laden with exposition ('The bomb will go off at midnight, Doctor Robin. Unless we can find the special six-inch spanner, the Cameron house will be blown sky high'). If you want to use dialogue as a way of conveying information to the reader, either the speaker must need to convey it, or the listener need to hear it, and preferably both.

Avoid smart alec repartee, or student banter, or any showing off at the reader's expense. Keep a short story collection near your desk for a range of examples of dialogue correctly laid out and punctuated.

Write a quarrel scene

Strong dialogue often conveys a character's will indirectly. Write a conversation between two women of different ages who are disagreeing about something minor: say, the relative merits of tea bags vs. leaf tea. But the discord between them goes deeper than that. Make sure that your reader will sense at least part of it.

PLOT

Because the short story lends itself to experimentation, there are many ways of approaching plot. Jane Smiley once played her creative writing students the first movement of Mozart's C major quintet, and said when it was over, 'Now you know all there is to know about writing a story.' She wanted her students' work to reproduce the 'tension between the desire to linger over the beautiful harmonies between the instruments, the equivalent of words, and the longing for the music to go forward, the equivalent of the storyline'.[11]

Raymond Carver also identifies tension as a key element of plot, but for him it comes from 'a sense that something is imminent, that certain things are in relentless motion'.[12] Keep the timescale tight, and do not overload your story with events. As Judith Leibowitz says, 'the novel's narrative task is elaboration, whereas the short story's is limitation'.[13] Plot can be described as the process by which you build up to the single incident or insight you wish to resonate in the mind of your reader. Do not distract her from this process by unnecessary scene-shifting.

Short stories are now more varied in theme and style than at any other point in their history. In your search for suitable structures, read the work of your favourite contemporaries, jot down their plots in your writer's journal, and adapt them to your own purposes. In 'All over the place',[14] for example, Michael Carson gives us 30 years of his heroine's life through the flotsam and jetsam of her travels, which include a scrawl in a school exercise book, a banker's draft, lines in a baptismal register, graffiti, and an inscription on a polished agate pendant. Michèle Roberts' 'Une Glossaire/A Glossary'[15] is a list of descriptions of people, places, food, furniture, clothes and events important to the narrator's life in France. Suniti Namjoshi reworks fables,[16] Salman Rushdie rewrites Urdu tales,[17] and Angela Carter and Emma Tennant update fairy stories, myths or classical legends. (For more ideas on this subject, consult Chapter 5, 'Working with myth'.) Sometimes writers such as Alice Munro produce a collection of short stories about the same characters which is marketed as a novel.[18] Other stories may be less a chain of events, and more a process of discovering where an image or sentence fits. Liam O'Flaherty's 'The Flood', for example, can be seen as a deepening of meaning by way of description.[19] A plot may even, as Joyce Carol Oates points out, 'be wholly interior, seemingly static, a matter of the progression of a character's thought'.[20] Though all plots need to develop and resolve themselves, in stories by Gertrude Stein and Samuel Beckett, for example, it is often language itself that metamorphoses. But remember that if you jettison recognizable characters and sharply dramatized scenes you will lose many readers who believe that character is plot, and plot character.

Experiment with story structure

Take a headline that intrigues you – say, IGUANA LOST IN CITY PARK. From whose point of view will you tell the story: the owner's, the iguana's, a terrified park-keeper's or a predatory taxidermist's? Will the tone be tense, surreal, descriptive, or meditative? What is the story really about, and what has changed by the end?

What to do if you are stuck for a plot

The traditional plot, first analysed by Aristotle, has recently been defined as 'a completed process of change'.[21] For Aristotle, successful stories have a beginning which introduces conflict, a middle section which develops it and an ending which resolves it.

If you cannot think of a plot, invent a protagonist (main character) who wants something – but not just to win the lottery, unless she will use the money to buy her Mongolian grandmother a ticket to Ulan Bator. Your reader needs a cause with which she can identify. Both Tremain's and Joyce's character-narrators, for instance, want something badly: Tremain's ex-businessman desires the love of his beautiful, mercenary wife, even though he knows he will never get it; and Joyce's young boy wants to buy a present at the bazaar for Mangan's sister. However small the thing that your character longs for, it must be important to her, as this gives a value to her actions. A limp main character can mean a boring story, so if your protagonist fails to come to life, try pushing her desire to an extreme. Then you will have the start of a plot. The questions you ask yourself about her motives will strengthen the portrait as your story unfolds.

Next you need what Aristotle called an antagonist, whose function is to stop your protagonist from getting what he or she wants. In your early attempts at the short story form it may be wisest to choose a human antagonist who gives you immediate scope for dialogue and interaction – two excellent 'hooks'; and remember to give your antagonist some of the best lines, otherwise your fiction will become propaganda.

The antagonist, however, does not have to be another character. Your protagonist may be thwarted by the weather, or romance, or sexual attraction, or by the habit of timorousness and gentility, as in Katherine Mansfield's 'The Daughters of the Late Colonel', or by his own lack of perception, like Gabriel in Joyce's 'The Dead';[22] or he could be up against a puzzle, like Edgar Allan Poe's detective in 'The Murders in the Rue Morgue'. In general, the bigger the obstacle, the stronger the desire, as when the prince sees the princess in the tower, or a shoplifter spots price-less jewellery locked in a display case fitted with alarms. From all these situations you can develop the kind of conflict which typifies many of the best stories from *The Iliad* to 'Snow White'.

Better to focus on small conflicts, and let them resonate in your char-acter's mind, and be keenly felt, than snatch at a huge issue and fail to develop it. For examples of momentous stories which hinge on small events, read Joyce's *Dubliners*, or any short story by Chekhov.

It is your job to make life hard for your characters at least some of the time, so make sure they do not get what they want straight away. Dramatize these obstacles, which are traditionally up to three in number. One setback shows the antagonist's power, the second builds tension and the third comes at the story's climax. When it comes to deciding on your setbacks, remember Jack M. Bickham's warning against confusing conflict with adversity. A character's dose of flu or cancelled train may serve to heighten the reader's sympathy, but bad luck can never take the place of 'give and take, manoeuvre, struggle and tension'.[23]

ENDING

Although many talented and successful writers have ignored or subverted the above guidelines, followed with flair they provide a reliable way of producing a readable short story with a choice of four basic endings: the protagonist gets what she wants and lives happily ever after, or realizes that her goal was not worth having; or she does not get what she wants, and it ruins her life; or else she finds out she was better off without whatever it had been in the first place.

There are, however, many other ways of ending a short story. Whichever one you choose, remember that it is your story's strongest statement, and because of the form's brevity it should in some way be contained in its beginning, like Ouroboros the snake with its tail in its mouth. The beginning of every story poses a question, if only obliquely, and your reader will feel cheated if your conclusion does not answer it. If your opening paragraphs lack direction, the resolution will probably be blurred.

The twist in the tail, made famous by the American, O. Henry, has gone out of fashion; but do not despise the revelation which can illuminate a whole story retrospectively, as in the last line of dialogue in Rudyard Kipling's 'The Gardener'.[24] Instead of rising to a climax, many modern short stories confine themselves to an acute realization in the mind of the central character: what Joyce defined as an epiphany, or moment of vision, as in the closing lines of his 'Araby': 'Gazing up into the darkness I saw myself as a creature driven and derided by vanity; and my eyes burned with anguish and anger.'[22]

Joyce Carol Oates believes that you need not end with a spelt-out statement, as long as you signal 'a tangible change of some sort; a distinct shift in consciousness, a deepening of insight'.[25] Today that change, she believes, can be confined to the reader's consciousness. Either way, make sure a change or a realization takes place, because without it there can be no story.

Notes

1 Introduction, *The Oxford Book of Short Stories*, quoted in 'Don Jacobson on the story of stories', *London Review of Books*, 19 May 1988.
2 Raymond Carver, 'On Writing', *Fires* (Picador, London, 1986).
3 Duncan Minshull (ed.), *Telling Stories*, vol. 3 (Sceptre, London, 1994).

4 Frank O'Connor, *The Lonely Voice: A Study of the Short Story* (Macmillan, London, 1963).
5 *The Penguin Book of Modern British Short Stories*, ed. by Malcolm Bradbury (Penguin, Harmondsworth, 1988).
6 David Evans, 'A Poetry Reading on Riverside', *Brought to Book: The Winners of the 1994 Ian St James Awards* (HarperCollins, London, 1994).
7 David Evans, 'Sabbatical', *Critical Quarterly*, vol. 30, number 1, spring 1988.
8 James Joyce, *Dubliners* (Penguin, Harmondsworth, 1967).
9 Graham Greene, *Twenty-One Stories* (Penguin, Harmondsworth, 1970).
10 James Friel, *A Posthumous Affair* (Pretext 2, EAS Publications, 2000).
11 Jane Smiley, 'A Bruch at Bedtime', *Guardian*, 12 February 1999.
12 Carver, 'On Writing'.
13 Quoted in Ian Reid, *The Short Story* (Critical Idiom series, Methuen, London, 1977).
14 In Minshull, *Telling Stories*, vol. 3.
15 Michèle Roberts, *During Mother's Absence* (Virago, London, 1993).
16 For example, Suniti Namjoshi, *The Blue Donkey Fables* (Women's Press, London, 1988).
17 For example, Salman Rushdie, 'The Prophet's Hair', in *The Penguin Book of Modern British Short Stories*.
18 For example, Alice Munro, *The Beggar Maid: Stories of Flo and Rose* (Penguin, Harmondsworth, 1980).
19 Liam O'Flaherty, *Irish Short Stories* (Penguin Audiobooks, Harmondsworth, 1998).
20 Joyce Carol Oates, 'Introduction', *The Oxford Book of American Short Stories* (Oxford University Press, Oxford, 1994).
21 R. S. Crane, quoted in David Lodge, *The Art of Fiction* (Penguin, Harmondsworth, 1992).
22 Joyce, *Dubliners*.
23 Jack Bickham, *Writing the Short Story: A Hands-On Programme* (Writer's Digest Books, Cincinnati, 1994).
24 Rudyard Kipling, *Twenty-One Tales* (The Reprint Society, London, 1946).
25 'Introduction', *Oxford Book of American Short Stories*.

7 WRITING FOR SCREEN AND TELEVISION

Dave Jackson

INTRODUCTION

Screenwriting is a form of creative writing which reaches millions of people every day. There will always be a demand for writers with the skill to tell stories economically and visually. Although most people think of Hollywood as the ultimate goal for screenwriters, British film and television currently offer considerable opportunities.

Screenplays are plans for proposed films or television programmes. They are not self-contained pieces of creative writing like poems, novels or short stories. Their purpose lies beyond the immediate words on the page. They are like blueprints for buildings still to be constructed. They are only the first stage of a collaborative process with producers, directors and actors.

During development, a screenplay may go through many changes and will remain *work in progress* until the film is finished. Films can cost enormous sums of money to produce and the chances of a screenwriter's original vision surviving the production process intact are slim. Perhaps this is why many successful screenwriters like Woody Allen, Jane Campion, Quentin Tarantino, Mike Leigh and Kevin Smith choose to direct their own work.

This is not meant to put you off screenwriting. While William Goldman in *Adventures in the Screen Trade*[1] urges aspiring screenwriters to find outlets such as poetry and novel writing for the frustrated creative urges that screenwriting will not satisfy, he also points out that for his first two novels he was paid a total of $7,500, while for his first Hollywood script he received $80,000. The point is simply that screenwriting can have a lot more to do with making money than it has to do with producing *art*. It is one of the few areas of creative writing where you stand a real chance of making a reasonable living and there is always the possibility of striking it rich.

If this appeals, it is important to get a real feel for your chosen craft. You need to watch and analyse as much film and television drama as you can and read lots of original screenplays. Many successful and unsuccessful screenwriters have written books on screenwriting. Most of them are American and most of them offer what may seem like formulaic approaches to the craft. These approaches, while varying in some respects, tend to agree on certain basic principles:

- 'a screenplay is a story told in pictures'[2]
- screenplays need structure
- screenplays deal with a central protagonist (sometimes a pair, less often a group)
- a screenplay's ending dictates its beginning.

You may think that this sounds restrictive, and you may prefer to ignore the 'rules' and adopt what you think is a more intuitive approach. Beware. Though you may be successful, it is more likely that you will make your task more difficult. You should at least have an understanding of what you are rejecting. Everyone in the film industry has absorbed these 'rules' and will ask questions such as, 'What is your inciting incident?' If you do not know what they are talking about, they may assume that you do not know anything about screenwriting.

What follows is a brief summary of some generally accepted principles of writing feature films, some related writing exercises and a short guide to screenplay layout. This will be followed by a briefer discussion of television writing, how it differs from cinema and a short guide to its various forms. For more detailed advice and discussion of what makes a good screenplay, you should consult some of the many books on the subject. Each writer has his or her own angle and it is worth considering as many different perspectives as possible.

VISUALIZATION

A screenplay deals with the external world in visual images. Novels can deal with the inner life of a character, explain their thoughts and feelings and detail their memories. Syd Field stresses that a screenplay is a story told in pictures. You must learn to think visually. Forget about dialogue for now. Dialogue comes last. Think instead about the ways in which films *show* rather than *tell* a story. Think about the openings of films that you like. How do they introduce you to their central characters and the worlds they inhabit?

Many films tell us a lot about a character, their world and their situation before a single word is spoken. A lot of films open with an establishing shot of the character's environment: the skyline of New York, for instance, or a strange planet seen from outer space. *East is East* opens with a Christian parade through the terraced streets of a northern English town. The clothing of the participants indicates that the film is set in the 1970s. Amongst the white marchers is a group of young Asians, laughing and carrying banners. Suddenly they panic. Their Muslim father has come out to watch the parade. They veer off down back alleys to avoid being seen, rejoining the parade only after it has passed him. This sets up the location, introduces the main characters, and tells us the central conflict of the film: the clash between the father's values and his children's. We receive most of this information visually.

Many films use colour and visual metaphor to convey information. In David Lynch's *Blue Velvet*, red and yellow flowers and a white picket fence against a too-blue sky introduce us to a suburban paradise, a palette of primary colours. A man waters his garden with a hose. But in darkness, beneath the grass, carnivorous insects engage in violent struggle. The hose becomes twisted, pressure builds. Suddenly the man has a stroke. Paradise is disturbed. The first time we see Jeffery, the central character, he is dressed in black, in sharp contrast to the colourful daylight world of Lumberton. He is already dressed to descend into the town's dark underworld when he finds the severed ear.

Another classic wordless opening sequence occurs in *Apocalypse Now*. An establishing shot shows a jungle tree-line. US army helicopters appear and explosions set the jungle on fire as the Doors play on the soundtrack. We know instantly that we are witnessing a scene from the Vietnam War. Then we see the next scene superimposed over the burning jungle. First his eyes, then the haggard upside-down face of the central character, Willard, lying on a bed, smoking a cigarette. The helicopters he has been dreaming about turn into the whirring blades of the ceiling fan. Exploring his messy room, we see a half-drunk bottle of whisky and a gun by his pillow. Even before it is confirmed in Willard's voice-over, we know he is a dangerous man.

Close your eyes and see ...

* Think about some of your favourite films and recall any scenes which had a strong visual impact. Think particularly in terms of colour and image. Think about the way these visual images are used to tell a story. Do different colours have different significance? It is no accident that the red shoes in the fairy tale eventually dance their wearer to death.

* Choose two colours. What images do these colours suggest? Maybe you think of blue and it suggests the sea, or the earth seen from space, and white, the colour of a space suit. Links will start to form in your mind – an astronaut returning from the moon to splash down in the Atlantic, perhaps.

> * Using your colours and images as springboards, write a few opening scenes for an imaginary film. Forget about dialogue completely. Think about metaphorical images – helicopter blades and ceiling fan, twisted hose and sudden stroke. Introduce a character and their world. Try to create an atmosphere and a sense of anticipation. Write in the present tense and describe only what you would see watching the action on a screen.

THE PREMISE

The premise is a crystallization of what your story is going to be about. Try to tell it in one or two sentences, at most a few paragraphs. Outline the most significant aspects of the drama. *The Matrix* is about Neo, a computer programmer, who discovers that he is living in a virtual world created by machines, learns he has the means to oppose them and sets out to liberate humanity from their control.

> **What is the genre?**
>
> * Pick five films you have seen and write short premises for them. Whose story is it and what is the story about? Try not to be side-tracked by subplots. Many detective stories, for example, also contain a love story but the real premise is about the solving of the crime.
> * Write several film premises of your own. Try different genres: a love story, a thriller, a comedy. Think in terms of a main character and the obstacles they must overcome. Give your character a name. Have fun. This is just an exercise in using your imagination.

THREE-ACT STRUCTURE

Many screenwriters and industry professionals maintain that most commercial feature films follow a *three-act structure*. Although there is no curtain or commercial break between acts, according to this notion feature films divide into three distinct parts: beginning, middle and end. While there are convincing arguments that no single all-embracing act structure can be applied to all narrative construction, this approach does have its merits. Try using this model, if only to see if it works for you.

Act 1

The beginning takes up approximately the first 20 to 30 minutes of a 120-minute screenplay. The first act is the base on which the following acts are built. It is where your story must be set up by introducing your main characters, the world they live in and the central problem which your protagonist must solve. An *inciting incident*, a dramatic event which upsets the balance of the protagonist's world in some way, setting the main story in motion, usually occurs within the first 10 minutes of act 1.

Most of the exposition occurs during this act and everything that happens in the middle and end relates to elements introduced here. The first act should build to some sort of a crisis – a major setback or revelation for your protagonist.

Though you need to hook the audience with your fascinating characters and central story problem as quickly as possible, be careful not to risk confusing the audience by introducing too many names and faces all at once. Introduce your characters gradually. Use established characters to introduce unknown characters. For example, in the first scene introduce Jack and Nicola. In the second scene Nicola leads us to her lover, Dave. In the third scene Jack goes for a drink with his two friends Bob and Paul. In three scenes five characters have been introduced, but because they have been introduced gradually, there is less chance of confusion than if all five appeared in scene 1.

Even in an ensemble film like *Pulp Fiction* which has multiple protagonists, Tarantino is careful to introduce us to characters one or two at a time. Tarantino is an example of a writer who understands film conventions so well that he can play around with them. In *Pulp Fiction* he deliberately breaks up the chronological order of events into three intersecting stories and reorders them into a non-linear story structure. Despite this, he still manages to achieve a definite feeling of beginning, middle and end.

Act 2

The middle should be the longest act of your screenplay, roughly 70 minutes of a 120-minute script. This is where the narrative develops and new problems start to build on the initial story problem. There should be a brief lull at the beginning of act 2, after the climax of act 1. Then you should slowly start to intensify the conflict and begin to develop subplots. A subplot is a secondary story strand which weaves in and out of your main storyline. Your main story is your protagonist striving after a goal; a policewoman on the trail of a clever serial killer, for instance. A subplot may grow out of that conflict. The policewoman develops a relationship with an incarcerated psychopathic genius in order to get an insight which will help her catch the killer at large. Your subplot characters are usually introduced in act 1, but their stories really start to develop in act 2.

You should start to develop new complications, building the conflict throughout act 2. It should climax at a much higher pitch of dramatic tension than the crisis that ended act 1.

Act 3

The end is the shortest act, taking up the final 20 minutes of a 120-minute script. This is where you draw your story to a conclusion and provide a sense of closure. The audience should feel it is right that your story ends where it does. This act should begin with another brief respite, when the tension that ended act 2 slackens off. But this is only the calm before the storm. Now the conflict should build quickly through a series of accelerating struggles to the climax of the film. This is the point of maximum tension, when your protagonist should either attain their goal or fail in the attempt.

After the climax, many films have a resolution scene where most plot ends are tied up, although a further question might be raised in the minds of the audience. The policewoman who has caught the serial killer may be at a congratulatory function when she receives a phone call from the now escaped psychopath, who sends his best wishes.

Looking at the three-act structure

- Watch films critically and see if they fit the dictates of three-act structure. Can you identify inciting incidents and the climax points near the ends of each act?
- Try breaking down a story you know well into three component acts – beginning, middle and end – bearing in mind the separate functions of each act, to establish, develop and conclude.

KNOWING YOUR ENDING DICTATES YOUR BEGINNING

Before you start writing your screenplay, you need to know how your story ends. You do not need to know the entire story in detail. But the end of your story dictates its beginning. If your hero is going to kill the villain with an unbelievable knife-throw at the end, it might be advisable to show that he used to be part of a circus knife-throwing act at the beginning. If you simply go ahead and write the script without knowing the ending, it is possible that a knife-throwing ending may arrive without any of the prefiguring that is going to make it seem plausible within the world of your film.

It is like setting out on a journey. If you have a destination in mind, you do not necessarily have to take the most direct route. You can detour to other places along the way, but your final destination will shape your journey. The end of your film shapes the elements you include in your script at the beginning. Robert Towne's *Chinatown* ends with the villain, Noah Cross, getting away with the murder of his son-in-law, the rape of his daughter and his involvement in a big water scandal, while the private detective protagonist, Gittes, watches helplessly. This ending is foreseen in a line in the very first scene where Gittes tells an enraged client, 'You've got to be rich to kill somebody, anybody, and get away with it.' Noah Cross is rich and he does get away with it.

The beginning of the end

Look at the endings of several films, say the last 10 minutes, on video or in script form. Then go back and look at the first 10 minutes. See if you can spot the set-ups that are dictated by the closing scenes. You should see the themes of the films emerge.

Practise writing a couple of ending scenarios. Think about the way these endings would affect the beginning of your imaginary films.

CHARACTER

Protagonist

The majority of films have one central character. This is the protagonist, the person whose story is being told: someone with a problem to solve. He or she wants something, but obstacles are put in the way by someone or something antagonistic towards the protagonist. Your story is about how the protagonist eventually overcomes the obstacles, or is overcome by them. Drama is about conflict and struggle.

In films with two or more protagonists, these central characters generally fall into one of two categories, what Robert McKee[3] calls the plural-protagonist and the multi-protagonist. In films with plural-protagonists the story is driven by two or more characters with a shared desire or goal. Examples are *Thelma and Louise*, *The Seven Samurai* and *The Dirty Dozen*. In films with multi-protagonists, the characters follow separate goals, and these films tell multi-plot stories. Films like *Pulp Fiction* and *Short Cuts* do this by interweaving several stories, each with its own central character.

Protagonists should have a powerful will which drives their need to achieve a goal. In *Blue Velvet*, Jeffrey's wilfulness drives the story. Finding the severed ear is the inciting incident which sets him on his investigative journey, but it is Jeffrey's wilful nature which makes him continue to pursue this investigation against the advice of the police.

As well as being wilful and having a strong conscious desire, protagonists often have an unconscious desire which may act against what they are supposed to want. In Neil Jordan's *The Crying Game*, the protagonist struggles over whether or not he can fulfil his role as an IRA agent, but we eventually discover that what he really wants is to love and be loved in return. In a discussion with some students about the film *Witness*, there was disagreement as to whether the main protagonist was John Book; the Amish boy, Samuel, who witnessed the murder; or his mother, Rachel. Although both Rachel and Samuel are introduced first, they prove to be the instruments that set John Book on the main physical and psychological journey of the story. The murder is presented to the detective as a problem for him to solve. His dramatic need or desire is to bring the killer to justice. This is thwarted at the end of the first act when, despite discovering the murderer's identity, Book is forced to go on the run with the Amish mother and child. The man behind the murder is his own boss. In the second act, Book enters the strange world of the Amish. It is here that he experiences a different set of conflicts, between his feelings and values and those of the religious community, which leave him a changed man at the end of the film.

Your central character should be someone in a state of perpetual physical or psychological motion, and needs to have the capacity to follow his or her desire to the end of the story. Protagonists should also engage the audience's sympathy. This recognition of shared humanity will enable the audience to identify with the character and want them to achieve their goal. In *Chinatown*, Gittes follows a trail of clues to discover who has murdered Mulwray, stolen water, and set him up as an unwitting dupe. Although Gittes is self-regarding and opportunistic, his flaws are portrayed in a manner which engages the audience's sympathy. Ironically, it is one of these character flaws, Gittes' reckless egotism, which plays him into the hands of his antagonist, Noah Cross, and causes Gittes to fail to save Evelyn Mulwray and her daughter.

Protagonists should change as a result of pressures exerted on them during your story. Always remember that drama is about conflict, and conflict often occurs when two characters have mutually exclusive aims. In this sense, every protagonist needs to be opposed. This is the role of the antagonist.

Antagonist

The antagonist may be a single individual or a combination of people whose purpose in the story is to frustrate the protagonist's attempts to achieve his or her goal. The antagonist does not have to be a villain. It may not even be a person. It could be anything: an evil scientist, an unscaleable mountain, a jealous ex-lover or an uncaring establishment. It may even be an aspect of the protagonist's own character, a fatal flaw which thwarts the character's attempts to achieve meaningful relationships. In Vincent Gallo's independent film *Buffalo 66*, the central character has to come to terms with his own anger and misdirected need for revenge before he can accept the love of Christina Ricci's character and come to terms with the world.

Although you should always strive to create believable, well-rounded characters, you should be aware that they all serve a function within the story, just as the protagonist's function is to pursue a goal. Many films include a character whose role is to function as the object of desire or 'love interest' for the protagonist. Also, the central character often has a confidante. This is someone the protagonist trusts and with whom they can drop their guard, showing vulnerability or other aspects of their character. This role could be taken by a partner who may even be a second protagonist.

Catalyst

The catalyst performs another important character function. He or she may be a witness to a crime who reports it to a detective, as Samuel does to John Book. It may be the British soldier who asks his IRA executioner to take a message to his girlfriend. Catalyst figures appear in almost every story. They serve to push the story forward and send the protagonist in new directions. They may only be minor figures and stories may have many catalysts.

Other characters

Films often have characters whose function is to provide comic relief, lightening the story by making the audience laugh. In *Notting Hill*, the Rhys Ifans character fulfils this function. Other characters may serve to highlight aspects of the protagonist's character through contrast. Thus a profligate protagonist may have a thrifty workmate, or a violent gangster may befriend a pious priest. Similarly, certain characters may be used to represent or express thematic concerns. In *Witness*, for instance, Eli represents the Amish non-violent way of life. You should, however, always strive to make these characters seem more than just functional. To do this, you need to get to know them thoroughly.

Character biographies

At the planning stage, you should make biographies of all your major characters. Try to describe in an impressionistic way how they look. Are they tall or short? Do not give specific height in feet and inches or physical details such as hair or eye colour, unless these details are important to the story. You do not want to limit unnecessarily the choice of actors for the role. You do, however, need to get a real sense of your characters' personalities.

Develop back-stories for your characters. What were they doing before your story began? Most importantly, how did events affect them emotionally? Describe their general outlook on life. This will govern their response. What inner conflicts are the characters controlled by, or trying to control? How do they respond to each other? You may want to write several pages on each character. Ask them questions. The more you know about your characters, the more credible they will become.

In the end, try to edit these descriptions down to just five or ten lines for major characters and three to five for minor ones. These condensed character biographies may be used as part of a treatment package.

Closer to home

Write a character biography of someone you know in one or two pages. Then edit it down. Try to convey their looks and personality traits in just 10 lines.

PLANNING

Before you write your screenplay, you need to plan its overall structure. *Scene cards, step outlines, treatments* and *outlines* are means to achieve this. At the planning stage, you should always write in the present tense. This is how your eventual screenplay will be written. The action is happening now. Avoid lapsing into the past tense.

Scene cards

Many writers put their basic scene ideas on index cards, using a separate card for each scene. In this way you can keep the story outline fluid and experiment with different juxtapositions of key scenes to see how this affects the dramatic structure of the whole. Using the model of the three-act structure, you could begin with cards representing the inciting incident and each of your act climaxes and slowly add and subtract scenes as you build a step outline around them.

Step outlines

A step outline tells the basic story in steps. It may be a simple list of key scenes, assembled from your scene cards, saying where each scene takes place, who is in it and briefly describing what happens. Though the step outline can be just a sequence of events, it could become a detailed scene-by-scene breakdown of the entire script and end up closely resembling a screenplay without the dialogue. This sort of detailed outline will make your final scriptwriting task much easier.

Treatment

A treatment is a screenplay told in story form and is usually between 2 and 15 pages long. At this stage you have the freedom to write in a more literary style, which may help in establishing the mood of your film. It should flow in logical order from beginning to end and should convey emotion as well as plot. Make it clear why your characters behave as they do, what impact events have on them, and vice versa. The treatment should give the subtext, the thoughts and feelings behind what is said and done. You can indicate what people talk about, but without including the dialogue.

The treatment can serve two functions. Firstly, it is a way of evaluating your story and characters before beginning the more detailed task of writing the script. You can see if your story makes sense and builds dramatically to its conclusion. By looking at the way one event relates to another, you can see if it has direction or wanders off at a tangent.

Secondly, the treatment can function as a detailed selling document which tells the story in full to potential agents and/or producers. Some writers are offered development deals on the strength of treatments alone, before they have written a word of the actual script. Think of your treatment as the blueprint for your screenplay in the same way that your screenplay will be a blueprint for a film. You can always change things. Like your screenplay, nothing in your treatment is set in stone.

The outline

The outline is a short treatment or synopsis which gives the premise, a basic outline of the plot and brief mention of the main characters. It should be between one and four pages long, and its main function is as a selling document to show to prospective agents and producers. Think of it as a review of a film not yet made. Outlines can be useful to gauge interest in a story idea before you turn it into a script or to promote interest in an existing screenplay. Some people in the industry insist on outlines or treatments before they will look at full scripts. Others prefer only to look at completed scripts, maintaining that an entertaining outline is no proof that an untried writer is capable of producing a good screenplay.

Outlining

Write an outline of a film you have seen recently.

FORMAT FOR SCREENPLAYS

Screenplays should be word processed in Courier 12-point and printed on a laser printer. Dialogue and visual directions should not be interrupted by page breaks.

Write in simple, functional language, avoiding florid descriptions or overly literary phrases. Be specific and precise. Keep to the present tense. The action is always happening now, as it appears on screen.

Only production scripts contain camera angles and editing directions. These should not appear in submission scripts. The only directions of this type you should include are FADE IN on the first page under the title on the left-hand side and FADE OUT two spaces down on the left-hand side after the last line of your screenplay.

This is the format for a submission script. Its purpose is to present the basic story. The director and not the writer decides how that story is interpreted on the screen. The three necessary elements in a screenplay are:

- scene heading (interior or exterior, location, time)
- visual exposition (what you would see if you were watching the screen)
- dialogue.

The scene heading states where the following action and dialogue is taking place, and tells us the time of day. It says whether this is inside (INT.) or outside (EXT.) The exact geographical location comes next, (LIVERPOOL) followed by the time of day (NIGHT). The scene heading is positioned on your first indent, 10 spaces in from the left-hand side of the page. Here is an example:

EXT. LIVERPOOL CITY CENTRE. NIGHT

Every time the action moves to another location you must give another scene heading. Each room in a house, for instance, constitutes a separate scene. Remember that you can enter a scene at any point. You may, for instance, choose to show only the end of an argument.

The visual exposition describes the action taking place on the screen and should only contain what you would see as a viewer of the film. The characters' names should be capitalized the first time they appear in the script, but not subsequently. The first time a character appears, the name should be followed by a short physical description including age and build, for example: 20-ish, wiry, ugly. The visual exposition should be beneath the scene heading at the same indent position, 10 spaces in from the left-hand side of the page. All lines should be single-spaced. For example:

MARNIE PEARSON, 30-ish, attractive, saunters into the room, looks around for a moment and then flops into an armchair, staring at her husband, EDWARD, late 40s, wiry, who stands looking out the window. He turns and glares at her. Marnie gives him a defiant smile.

No explanation is given why Edward glares or Marnie smiles. The reasons for their behaviour will be revealed through their actions and dialogue. It is not necessary to include motivational explanations such as: Edward, angry at his wife's infidelity, looks mad. This should be revealed later in dialogue.

Dialogue should follow the visual exposition, with the character's name capitalized in the centre of the page. The words spoken follow on the next line, indented, with the left and right margins about 20 spaces in from each side of the page:

MARNIE
God! You're ugly when you frown.

DIALOGUE

Film dialogue is not real-life conversation. It should not meander aimlessly, the way that most everyday conversation does. It should be economical and resonant. Lines should be short and spare. Try not to give one character more than three or four lines of dialogue at a time. If a character is giving a long speech, try and break it up either by interjections from other characters or by inserting bits of relevant visual exposition. This stops the script looking dialogue-heavy.

Make different characters speak differently, with different rhythms, different uses of language and different sentence lengths. Their speech patterns and what they say should reveal things like cultural background, educational level and age.

Your characters should speak for themselves rather than just act as conduits for information that you want to give to the audience. A certain amount of expository dialogue is inevitable, but it should be disguised or distracted from by having something else going on at the same time.

People do not always tell the truth and quite often say the opposite of what they really mean. The subtext of the story is what is going on behind the dialogue, the way a waiter in a restaurant may wish a customer 'Good evening, sir', while making an exasperated face at one of his colleagues. In film you can show a lot of non-verbal communication. So avoid stagy proclamations and, wherever possible, tell the story with action rather than words. Always remember, show, don't tell.

Creating dialogue

⊛ Look at everyday situations, at the disparity between what people say and what they do. See how subtexts emerge out of conversations which appear to be about something else altogether.

⊛ Write a situation where two people talk while doing something *everyday*, like shopping or working. One of the characters wants to bring up something he or she feels it important they discuss. The other character keeps trying to steer the conversation in another direction. Give the two characters different speech patterns. See what you can reveal about them, as much by what they do not say as what they do.

WRITING FOR TELEVISION

While feature films are intended to be viewed by static audiences watching cinema screens, television programmes are geared to small-screen domestic viewing, where the viewer may be doing other things while watching. Television narratives are often interrupted by commercial breaks or broken into episodes. On one level, viewing is less concentrated than the cinema experience. On another, it can be more intimate and ongoing, as reflected by the type of dramatic storytelling that seems best suited to the medium. Long-running series and soap operas with their repetitive and continually interweaving plots, with no resolution, dominate the schedules.

Television narratives are generally more dialogue-driven than those of the feature film. The scale of events is usually smaller and the dramatic situations more domestic. Fewer characters can appear on the small screen in any one scene. The cinema's wide screen shows wonderful crowd scenes: but four is a crowd on television.

SHORT FILMS

These tend to be shown late at night on either BBC2 or Channel 4, and rarely get a cinema screening except at specially organized festivals. There is currently, however, a renewed interest in short films. Primarily, they seem to function as show-reels for new directors, but they also offer writers a chance to demonstrate their skill. Channel 4's *Short and Curlies* season was specifically designed to encourage new writers.

The short short is usually under five minutes long and tends to have the plant and pay-off structure of a joke. An example of this sort of narrative is Eric Christiansen's *I Mean It*, made for Film Four's *Shooting Gallery* season.

A husband watches his wife tie the front of her jogging shorts, telling her he suspects she is having an affair. She tells him not to be stupid and goes out for a run, during which she meets her lover in his van. As she pulls her clothes back on, the lover asks her if she has told her husband yet. She says she could not. She has realized she still loves him. The lover kicks her out of the van. Back home, she tells her husband they should go on a second honeymoon together. The husband goes to hug her but she says she needs a shower and turns to go to the bathroom. Suddenly the husband starts sobbing. While his wife wonders what is wrong, we see that the drawstring on her shorts is at the back.

ONE-OFF DRAMAS

Many older television writers and producers bemoan the demise of the single play. According to producer Tony Garnett, 'During one year in the middle of the sixties we put out thirty-four original full-length single dramas each between 75 minutes and 100 minutes long.' This was where a new generation of writers such as Dennis Potter and Ken Loach first rose to prominence. One-off single dramas made for television are scarce these days. Jimmy McGovern's *The Dockers* is one of the few exceptions that springs to mind.

SERIALS

Serial dramas consist of one complete story told over several episodes. There could be as few as three or as many as 12 instalments. They are usually written by a single writer and have the same overall creative continuity as a single drama or a feature film, but with a wider scope. Many serials are adapted from well-known novels, such as *Brideshead Revisited*, *A Dance to the Music of Time*, *Pride and Prejudice* and *Gormenghast*.

Writers such as Lynda La Plante, Jimmy McGovern and the late Dennis Potter have produced original serial dramas like *The Singing Detective*, *Lipstick on my Collar*, *Killer Net*, *Lonesome Dove*, *The Thorn Birds*, *Shogun*, *Prime Suspect* and *Cracker*. Stories like *Gormenghast* are ideally suited to the serial form, as its director Andy Wilson says: 'It doesn't have a movie structure ... It's a saga and with sagas you need space to expand.' Serial drama gives the audience time to live with the characters and can easily accommodate multi-protagonist stories.

DRAMA SERIES

Series are collaborative productions. They use rotating teams of writers and directors but endeavour to maintain a house style. Series feature the same core of characters and settings in every self-contained episode. This means that the audience becomes familiar with a group of characters, but can watch episodes in isolation without having to follow cliff-hanging plotlines.

However, series often incorporate serial elements into their storylines. This means that while a single episode of *ER* may tell a couple of self-contained stories, it will have other storylines involving the regular characters which continue throughout the series. These are known as serial story arcs, and can also be seen in series such as *The X-Files* which involves government conspiracy, as well as each episode's story.

Examples of long-running series which together with soap operas make up the bulk of television's dramatic programming are: *The Bill*, *London's Burning*, *The Cops*, *City Central*, *Hill Street Blues*, *Homicide*, *The Sopranos*, *NYPD Blue*, *Hercules* and *Buffy the Vampire Slayer*.

SOAPS

Soaps are multi-protagonist serials which never end, mimicking real life. Their actors age with the characters they play. British soaps include *Coronation Street*, *EastEnders*, *Brookside*, *Emmerdale* and *Family Affairs*.

For many writers, soaps or drama series like *Casualty* and *The Bill* offer the most likely route to paid employment. Jimmy McGovern, writer of film and television dramas such as *Priest*, *Hillsborough*, *Cracker* and *The Dockers* began his professional writing career with *Brookside*. Frank Cottrell Boyce, writer of *Butterfly Kiss* and *Welcome To Sarajevo*, wrote for *Coronation Street*. Tony Jordan, creator of the police series *City Central*, was given his first break on *EastEnders*.

Generally, soaps have regular storylining sessions in which future events are worked out and broken down into episode storylines. These storylines are given to individual writers who then write the episode, bearing in mind considerations of continuity. *Brookside*, for instance, has a team of up to 12 writers who attend regular storylining sessions. *Family Affairs* has a separate team of storyliners who provide their writers with such detailed scene-by-scene breakdowns that their job is to provide dialogue rather than plot.

Writers' creative freedom varies from soap to soap and probably with the status of the writer. Soaps, like long-running series, have an ever-evolving document called a Bible which writers can refer to. This contains a list of episodes to date, what has been covered in them and biographies of the characters. If the series revolves around a specialized area like the police force or the medical profession, the Bible will include details of procedure and organizational structure.

Potential writers may be asked to submit a sample of their work. Then they may be offered the opportunity to write a trial script. This can take different forms. *Brookside* asks writers to produce half an episode with a limited number of characters and locations on a theme the script editor or producer suggests over the phone. They will expect you to display familiarity with the characters and their current storyline and you will be given a limited time to produce it. *Family Affairs* gives rookie writers a copy of a full episode outline to translate into scenes and dialogue.

SITCOMS

Situation comedies are generally 30 minutes long and, in common with drama series, feature a small core of characters in each self-contained episode. Within these characters there is usually either one whose story dominates, determining the course of action, e.g. Blackadder in *Blackadder* and Basil in *Fawlty Towers*, or there is a conflicting character relationship which dominates the action, e.g. Niles and Frasier in *Frasier*. Sitcoms usually take place in one or two central locations. If the show becomes very successful, the number of locations may grow. The writer's aim is to generate humour from the characters' attempts to confront their problems and deal with each other. This, with a few exceptions such as *Mr Bean*, is mainly done through dialogue. Examples of situation comedy are: *The Royle Family*, *Father Ted*, *Ellen*, *Roseanne*, *Dad's Army*, *Friends*, *Steptoe and Son*, *Larry Sanders* and *Seinfeld*.

CONCLUSION

Writing for screen and television is a collaborative art, so you will need to cultivate from the outset a willingness to revise and redraft your work: to see your script as only part of a process, not a completed product.

Scriptwriting may enable you to reach a wider audience than any other medium, but the competition is fierce.

Do not be afraid of involving yourself in the production side: it can only enhance your understanding of the writing process. Identify local companies and producers whose work you admire and send them your script. Cultivate any contacts. Today's local television producer may be tomorrow's Tarantino.

Perhaps more than any other kind of writer, the person who submits their work to a production company or television channel needs to be professional, determined, and immune to discouragement.

Good luck!

Notes

1 William Goldman, *Adventures in the Screen Trade* (Abacus, New York, 1984).
2 Syd Field, *Screenplay* (Dell Publishing, New York, 1982).
3 Robert McKee, *Story* (UK Methuen, London, 1999).

8 WRITING POETRY

Gladys Mary Coles

'Poetry is not the thing said but a way of saying it.'

A. E. Housman

WHAT IS POETRY?

Poetry is not only a way of saying but a way of seeing, and an art of
suggestion in which language is at its most intense and magical. Poetry is
form. Poetry is the shaping of language into special patterns that will
bring out more pleasure, more meaning. A 'poem' without a deliberately
chosen form is not a poem, it is a mess of words.

The most important way that poetry is patterned, or formed, is in
sound. Poetry is, after all, designed to be read aloud. The way that sound
forms regular and recognizable patterns is known as rhythm, from a
Greek word meaning flow or movement. Rhythm is a principle of life,
from our own beginnings in the womb, our breathing and heartbeats, to
the solar system, the movement of planets, the cycle of tides and seasons.
Around us are pulses and rhythms of all kinds. T. S. Eliot spoke of poetry
beginning with primitive man beating his drum, with dance and incanta-
tion, structured around rhythmic repetition. Nursery rhymes captivate
us in early childhood because we respond to the sound, the strong
rhythm and rhyme, which also facilitate memorizing and chanting. All
poems have rhythm (the rise and fall of words). It is essential to have a
grasp of rhythm if you want to write poetry – otherwise your work may
look like poetry on the page, but sound like prose when it is read aloud.
Regular rhythm can help to project a message or theme, and traditional
forms such as the ballad or the sonnet use 'set' patterns of rhythm
(though once you are skilled in the regular rhythm, you can begin to
experiment with slight variations). This chapter only begins to cover the
forms available to the poet. More can be learned from such works as
Lewis Turco's *The New Book of Forms: A Handbook of Poetics*,[1] and Sandy

Brownjohn's *Does It Have to Rhyme?*[2] There is a whole world of forms – enough for a lifetime – and poetry is the apprenticeship of a lifetime. But every choice you make about word order, rhyme, line breaks and images, must be a deliberate one, an informed one; one that shows awareness of the effect your poem will have on your reader.

Metre

When you hear poetry the rhythm works on you unconsciously, and you do not have to describe the sound pattern; only feel its effects. When you come to study or write poetry, however, and discuss the rhythm with other poets, you need a common language, a common means of measuring or describing sound. We call this metre (from the Greek word to measure). In English, some syllables receive more force, or stress, than other syllables – they are pronounced more fully. In the word 'second-hand', for example, we clearly hear the first syllable, 'sec' but the next syllable, when the word is said naturally, shrinks to a brief, unimportant sound – more like '-nd' than 'ond'. In the word 'jagged', the first syllable, 'jag', sounds heavier or more emphasized than the second syllable, 'ud'. In both these cases we refer to the first syllable as *stressed*, the second, 'lighter', 'smaller' one as *unstressed*. In poetry, rhythm is created by the arrangement of stressed and unstressed syllables at regular intervals in a line, so that 'heavy' and 'light' sounds develop a regular beat, similar to the way in which music establishes a beat – '*one* two three four'. Metre, therefore, is the formal description of the patterns of stressed and unstressed syllables in a line. Poetry differs from prose in that its rhythm is deliberately controlled to create meaningful and pleasurable effects.

Iambs

The most widely used rhythm in English poetry is *iambic metre*: this is the one which most closely approximates to the rhythms of English speech. It consists of one unstressed syllable followed by a stressed one, and so on through the line. In pronouncing the English language the stresses often fall naturally into single *iambs* or units of iambic metre, as in the following words (stresses capitalized):

dePART toDAY aBOUT deFLECT upSET reCALL

Some longer words form two iambs, that is, two units of an unstressed followed by a stressed syllable: riDICuLOUS, adMONishMENT, relTerATE, as do some phrases: 'to HEAR the SOUND', 'go THROUGH the GATE'. It is possible for whole sentences to accidentally fall into iambic metre, as in 'I HAD to GO inSIDE to GET a COAT' or 'He COMES there EVery MORNing AFter TWELVE'. Say these aloud and you will hear the rhythm. Five iambs (sometimes known as iambic feet) make a line of iambic pentameter. As each iamb has two syllables, there are ten syllables in the line, alternately stressed and unstressed. For example, from Thomas Gray's 'Elegy in a Country Churchyard',

> The CURfew TOLLS the KNELL of PARTing DAY,
> The LOWing HERD winds SLOWly O'ER the LEA

The measured pace of the metre, sustained throughout, imbues the poem with a strong sense of inevitability. In Christina Rossetti's sonnet, 'Remember', iambic pentameter creates the slow pace appropriate to the sad theme:

> Remember me when I have gone away
> Gone far away into the silent land

The poet's task, simply put, is to arrange her words so that a pleasing or regular metre is formed, and so that the stress falls on the syllables which are most important to her meaning. Once the rhythm has been established, it is possible to vary it for creative effect.

THE BALLAD

The ballad is a simple but enduring form which uses a strong rhythm. Ballads are narrative poems, which tell a story, often a melodramatic story of tragedy, love, murder or haunting; and they are always strongly rhythmic and lyrical. The traditional ballad is arranged in four-line verses (or quatrains) in lines of alternating metre, with four iambs, and hence four stressed syllables, in lines 1 and 3, and three iambs, and thus three stressed syllables in lines 2 and 4, and with the second and fourth lines rhyming. Here is a verse from 'The ballad of Sir Patrick Spens'.

> The king sits in Dumferling toune,
> Drinking the blude-reid wine:
> 'O whar will I get guid sailor,
> To sail this schip of mine?'

RHYME SCHEMES

Rhythm is one way in which sound becomes pleasantly patterned. The other chief way is rhyme. Rhyme is intrinsic to the musicality of poetry and to the creation of particular effects. It can support mood and meaning, give emphasis, and be an aid to fixing the poem in the memory, as in William Blake's 'The Tyger':

> Tyger! Tyger! burning bright
> In the forests of the night

Just as you can use metre to describe the rhythm of the line, you can use a rhyme scheme to describe the rhyming sounds. This is a traditional way of organizing your poem, using a pattern of end rhymes; letters are used to notate each sound. The letter is repeated each time the same sound is employed as is shown alongside the following quatrain, or four-line verse.

I have desired to go	a
Where springs not fail,	b
To fields where flies no sharp and sided hail	b
And a few lilies blow.	a

Gerard Manley Hopkins, 'Heaven-Haven'

Full and half rhyme

Ballads use full rhymes – repetition of the final sound of the words, as in sound/bound, cross/moss, arts/parts. Such rhyming at the end of lines, in regular stanza patterns (rhyme schemes) was once thought to be essential if a piece was to be regarded as poetry. The English language is not rich in full rhymes, and overuse has made many combinations sound hackneyed, e.g. moon/croon, night/bright. A full rhyme in a poem sets up an expectancy of echo which the ear desires to be fulfilled. The effect is satisfying, particularly in humorous and satiric verse (the limerick, for example), or in modern forms such as rap lyrics, which often use couplets (two-line stanzas) with an **aa bb cc** rhyme scheme.

Poets today have many other options apart from full rhyme. Half rhyme is when the two rhyming words have different vowel sounds but identical final consonants: Kill/sell, most/mast. It is a subtle sound technique, giving greater flexibility than full rhyme, effective in imbuing a poem with emotional undertones and resonance. Wilfred Owen used half rhyme as end rhyme systematically in his war poetry to create a sense of disturbance, e.g. ground/grind; loads/lids/lads; hall/Hell. Consider the effect of such discords in Owen's poem, 'I am the Enemy you Killed, my Friend':

> I knew you in this dark: for so you frowned
> Yesterday through me as you jabbed and killed.
> I parried; but my hands were loath and cold.

Owen made lists of half rhymes in preparation for writing poems. Such pairings help to train the ear and can work at a subconscious level. Try making your own lists in your journal – but do not feel you have to cram them all into a single poem.

Rhymes in action

Choose two rhyme schemes from poems you have read and compose a poem using each scheme. When you have done this, experiment. Create your own rhyme schemes. Try varying your rhyming techniques, using full rhymes and half rhymes. Be consistent, sustaining your scheme all through the poem.

Dangers to avoid

Watch out for predictable rhymes or heavy forced rhymes which dominate a poem, attracting attention to themselves. Any rhyme that can be guessed in advance is too heavy. Good rhyming is unobtrusive. Pair words which have an element of surprise. Never distort the natural order of speech, contorting your syntax to produce the rhyming word at the line's end, or sacrifice sense in the pursuit of a rhyme.

Internal rhyme and alliteration

Rhyming (or half rhyming) words need not occur in the most obvious position at the end of a line. They can be placed anywhere *within* the line or lines of a poem, creating an echo or chime. This internal rhyming enhances the verbal music of the poem, and can amplify the tone and emphasize meaning. It also has binding power, giving the poem a sense of unity and cohesion, which is useful in free verse (see below). For example:

> he loved her like that, her black gloves in the rain
> tight boots for nightclubs, the pain she left

Here *love* and *glove*, *tight* and *night*, rhyme in a way that is subtle enough to set up an echo without drawing attention to themselves as they would at the end of the line. *Pain* and *rain* make a more distant relationship between the two lines, but still illustrate the connection of threads of sound that can give the ear pleasure, and help to orientate the reader towards threads of meaning woven through a poem.

Note the way that the stresses in these lines, while not obeying a regular set pattern, draw attention to key points of meaning. In the first line stress falls on *love, black, glove* and *rain*. Say the lines out loud and see if you can spot the stresses and see how they point up the meaning of the second line.

A less obvious form of sound patterning, but one still popular in contemporary poetry, is *alliteration*, the repetition of a single consonant sound in the same line or cluster of lines. Two or more consonants can be used to give multiple alliteration, as in:

> Only the stuttering rifles' rapid rattle
> Can patter out their hasty orisons.
>> *Wilfred Owen*, 'Anthem for Doomed Youth'

THE SONNET

The sonnet is the most popular of the traditional forms. With 14 lines of iambic pentameter, it combines brevity with depth. The sonnet is versatile in its capacity to debate many subjects beyond the traditional ones of love, death and transience. While its roots are very old, the sonnet is still a popular form with contemporary writers from Carol Ann Duffy to R. S. Thomas, and employed to reflect on a huge range of topics. The Italian derivation of the name, 'little song', suggests its lyrical quality, the music of its metrical lines and rhymes. The Petrarchan or Italian sonnet has an **abba cddc efefef** rhyme scheme. The Shakespearean or English sonnet is organized in three quatrains and a closing couplet of iambic pentameter. Its rhyme scheme is: **abab cdcd efef gg**.

The development of a thought or argument is built up here in three separate stages through the three quatrains, and then resolved in the last two lines, the rhyming couplet having a clinching effect, often being an epigrammatic summing up, as in this example:

> For sweetest things turn sourest by their deeds;
> Lilies that fester smell far worse than weeds.
>> *William Shakespeare*, Sonnet XCIV

Poets first attempting a sonnet sometimes feel constrained by the strong scheme of end rhymes to write a poem of 14 end-stopped lines, each one almost self-contained and stopping at the rhyme, but this can lead to a stilted effect. Try enjambement (from the French for 'to step over'), running your sense on through the line break into the next line, as here:

Devon Churches

> You keep looking for it, a place so still
> that after the door's echo you can hear
> a lark, a tractor fields away, aisles filled

with the cold quiet shock of others' prayer:
that pause. The saints in the late August
sun bleeding scarlet stains across the face
of an unplastered wall, the lingering hush
of dying lilies. As though some other place
were near, held between breaths, as in the glass,
Adam is held in the red clench of scales;
as though in the damp book you'd find, at last
a cryptic hint of some elusive grail,
the confirmation of this search: some guide,
some word or name, a sign you recognize.

Edmund Cusick

Read this poem aloud. Hear its rhythm. None of these lines except the last one ends with a full stop, but lines 4 and 10 are nonetheless end-stopped – that is, the sense comes to a pause with the line break. Such pauses at line breaks serve to slow the poem down (see the section on punctuation below), whereas the enjambement at the end of lines 2 and 5, for example, serves to drive the poem on. The rhyme scheme employs both half and full rhyme, though the lack of full rhyme to close the poem suggests questions that remain unresolved, a closure not fully achieved.

Note the use of internal half rhyme – the softest, least obtrusive form of rhyme – in fields/ filled saints/stains, and the continuous thread of sound woven by the 'l' sound. How does the sound connect with the meaning?

SYLLABICS

Some poems are structured not according to the number of stressed syllables, but according to the number of all the syllables. The most well known of these forms is the three-line Japanese form, the haiku. Brief and economic, it is usually unrhymed and is not metrical. There are 17 syllables, the first line having five syllables, the second line seven, the third line five. The spirit of this form lies in its open-endedness, the reverberations it sets up through the image it presents, and the intense perception (traditionally of nature, the seasons and the universe) caught in a single picture.

In the dawn a pale
leaf trembles before the sun
light steals its shadow.

> **Haiku**
>
> Write several haiku based on scenes you know intimately: for example, the view from your window.

FREE VERSE

It may seem hard at first to follow set patterns such as iambic pentameter; but it is much harder to invent completely new metrical forms which are both pleasingly rhythmic and direct the ear, through stress, to the meaning you, the poet, wish to 'illustrate' through sound. Free verse is, therefore, the hardest poetry of all to write if you are a beginner. The term 'free-form' or free verse is often misunderstood – it involves the freedom to invent your own form, a responsibility entailing hard – but enjoyable – work in deciding every line break, every stanza break, every line length, and every use of stress, working out which shape on the page will help your meaning best. It does not, as beginners have sometimes imagined, mean the freedom not to have a deliberate form, but to spill words at random across a page. This may be fun, but disorganized prose is not poetry, and will soon bore or tire your reader. Poetry is far more highly organized than prose – professional poets sometimes take dozens of drafts to get a single page of poetry 'right'. While you want to reach a wide audience, it is good to have in mind your ideal reader – someone who loves poetry, and so knows a great deal about it, and understands the beauty and subtlety of poetic form. In terms of craftsmanship, there is a sense in which poets are always writing for other poets. Every reader will, ideally, be moved by what you write: only another poet will fully appreciate the technique which underlies your work.

Free verse is usually not used with full rhyme or end rhyme. Internal rhyme, however (often involving half rhyme), can bind the poem together giving a charge and emotional colouring. Free-form poetry demands the arranging of sound patterns in each line according to the precise effect that you wish that line to create.

Each free-verse poem you write will have its own individual and inherent structure. With practice you will learn intuitively to shape your lines – to lineate – subtly, for flow, surprise and emphasis. In free-form poetry the controlling factor is the line break. You need to be aware exactly where and why you are ending a line and beginning a new one; otherwise your poem will seem to be merely chopped-up prose.

The purpose of a line break is often to sustain tension and interest, using the last word on your line as a springboard to the next line, making your reader want to read on. Do not let your line sag at the end with 'a', 'the' or a weak preposition, such as 'for', 'with', or 'by'. For example:

> He came, with a basket of gifts, fish for the
> women to cook

This first line ends limply; it can be strengthened by re-arrangement:

> He came, with a basket of gifts, fish
> for the women to cook

If you are end-stopping, the pause at the end of the line must, like all your technical decisions, be for a good reason: perhaps a comma indicating the natural breathing pause between phrases (you will hear this when reading your work aloud), or a full stop ending a sentence or phrase and giving a sense of completion before the poem moves on to another image. Do not end-stop too often as it kills flow. Use enjambement, flowing from one line to the next, even perhaps from one stanza to the next.

Line breaks

Consider these lines of a poem 'Across the Berwyns', written out as prose:

> Snowfall slither. A warning on the sign at the bottom of the B road climb. I'm seeking the ice plateau, need, after fire, the salving of snowscapes, white silence.

Write this out as poetry, choosing where to make line breaks. Some hints: the poet chose to bring in an element of danger in the first line. Can you hear a half rhyme? The poet used it as a binding device between two lines presenting danger. One sentence flows across three lines. There is a surprising image there, too.

When you have done this, try taking a poem in free form and writing it out, without its line breaks, as prose. Then write the poem out again, placing line breaks where you think they should be. Compare your version with the original. You will now have two poems, similar but not identical in the meanings they create. Think about the different effects of the different line breaks. Then take one of your own poems and try the same exercise. It is much easier to do this, literally at the touch of a button, on a word processor.

PUNCTUATION

With the absence of the preordained rhythm of traditional verse forms, you assume responsibility for the speed at which your poem moves. Move too slowly and you will bore the reader, move too quickly and they will be confused, or miss the subtle points you wished them to guess at. The speed of a poem is controlled in part by its line breaks, but also by its punctuation. A comma indicates a slight pause. The full stop indicates a longer pause. The semi-colon and colon are somewhere in between the two. The decision of how many sentences to divide your poem into – how many full stops to use – can be crucial in its effect on your readers, even though it is one which happens unconsciously, without the reader knowing how they are being directed.

Judging your speed

Copy a poem you enjoy, and delete its punctuation. Then repunctuate it yourself. Compare the two poems, and see if you can judge why the poet made the decisions that she did. Try varying the punctuation in your own poems, and judging the effects.

In deciding what form to use, be guided by your subject matter. Consider the content carefully. If your poem is not working, it may be because the form is inappropriate. Allow the form to evolve from the subject or theme at the heart of the poem, rather than imposing a form upon it.

TITLES

Titles are an intrinsic part of your poems, not labels. They should not only be apposite, but hint at the content, create expectation. They can intrigue too, but should not be misleading or showy. They can set the tone of the poem and/or give information important to an understanding of it such as indications of place and period. In some cases the title acts as the first line, as in

Leafburners

move quietly as smoke

An untitled poem is a lost opportunity. It gives the impression of a failure of inspiration, or of a lazy poet.

Titling

Read through the index or contents pages of a poetry anthology. Write down all the titles which make you want to read a poem, and all those that definitely make you want to avoid one! What makes them effective? Consider the titles of some poems by your favourite poets. What relationship do they bear to the subjects of the poems? Then look back at your own titles, and see if they can be improved. Try a few alternative titles to the same poem, and see what response you get from your readers.

FIRST LINES, FIRST DRAFTS

As you begin to compose your poem, do not worry about the first line; do not let it hold you up, do not struggle for perfection. The process is like uncorking a bottle of wine – the hardest bit is getting it moving. Let your poem flow – the first line might well be one which you edit out eventually, but you need to write it to get the poem flowing. The main consideration is to keep going until you have run out of 'inspiration'. Always read your poems aloud as you are drafting them. This will give you the feel of all aspects of your language: the tone, movement and rhythm, the pace and the pauses. With set metrical forms, do not force yourself to get every rhyme and stress right first time – it is probably impossible, anyway. Get a first draft down, and then work at it, shaping words as a sculptor shapes clay or marble, gradually getting closer and closer to the form she desires.

All sorts of language can find expression in poetry – poetry can be an ice rink on which words can both play and dance – but never use words because you think they sound poetic. The worst examples are old-fashioned phrases: 'thees' 'thous' and other archaisms, and poeticisms such as 'wondrous', 'morn' and 'blest'. Such language even at its best sounds out of date; at its worst it will make your poem seem clichéd and insincere, because its words are transparently secondhand.

The guideline in all forms of imaginative writing, 'show rather than tell, illustrate rather than state', is no less important in poetry. Aim for illustration through sensory detail: you will then be using particulars which are 'concrete' (real, tangible, material detail), and with which your reader can connect: concrete words such as dog, onion, sour, bridge, munch, spindly, tang, waterfall, howl. Avoid abstract words (such as despair, hope, honour, love, peace, beauty). Abstractions are vague, generalizing, and should be avoided. Always aim to be specific rather than to generalize. For example, instead of using the word 'fruit', specify what kind of fruit; rather than the word 'beauty', show in what way something is beautiful. Death in general is hard to communicate, but a particular death, presented through that of a single named person, individualized by detail, will be more convincing.

Lists

Write a poem based on a list. Choose a subject which interests, intrigues or even repels you. For one possible example look at Carole Satyamurti's poem 'Mouthfuls' which focuses in sensory detail on various types of sweets enjoyed in childhood such as sherbet lemons: 'vicious yellow' whose 'sugar splinters lacerate'. While evoking the sweets, the poet is at the same time evoking her own childhood, and connecting to the memories of many of her readers. Make your images as tangible, as concrete, as possible.

IMAGERY

The creation and crafting of images is of central importance in writing poetry. An image is a picture conveyed to the reader's mind. All the senses can be drawn on to create imagery, not only sight. As a poet you can think and feel through your images. They should not be showy, drawing attention to themselves. As defined by Aristotle, a good metaphor 'implies the intuitive perception of the similarity in dissimilar'. The art is to see a common quality underlying two quite disparate things, bringing them together to create an arresting image. Similes are comparisons that use the words 'like' or 'as' – they make an imaginative link between two things, but keep them separate: for example, 'when the evening is spread out against the sky / like a patient etherized upon a table' (T. S. Eliot, 'The Love Song of J. Alfred Prufrock'). Similes are one of the most popular poetic devices, entering common speech in expressions such as 'wet as an otter's pocket'. Metaphor collapses this distance, uniting the two things compared, as in 'the glossy black cocoon of her PVC dress'. It is in this transformation that the power of metaphor lies. Metaphor redefines, sees something fresh in the ordinary, everyday world, defamiliarizing the familiar, fusing two dissimilars by giving one the properties of the other. Do not strain after your comparisons, forcing the images.

In Sylvia Plath's 'Daddy' she refers to her father as

> a black shoe
> In which I have lived like a foot
> For thirty years,

a metaphor which encloses a simile.

A poem reverberates by means of a pattern of images which refract each other and interrelate: the pattern is also part of the structure and meaning. In my poem 'As Mad As a Hatter's Child' various images of roundness (bowler hats, barrels, horses' flanks, men's stomachs, bonnets) reflect the key image of pregnancy and also evoke the nineteenth-century world of this poem with its theme of the deaths of hatters' babies and young children.

VOICE

The distinctive voice resonating through your work will emanate from many elements – your diction, rhythm, use of language, phrasing, handling of syntax; and also from your subject matter, your vision, your individual way of thinking and saying.

Your own life is the obvious starting point for poetry. As you grow in experience as a poet, you will probably wish to step out of a narrow auto-biographical range and write poems which explore other characters' experiences. Sliding inside the mind and personality of another person or character, just as in fiction and scriptwriting, you project your poem from their point of view, stance and situation. Paradoxically, one way to find your own voice is to practise imaginatively writing 'through' other people – the ways in which you bring their experience to life will tell readers about you, even though you do not intend it to. The dramatic monologue is a poem told from the point of view of a specific character, often drawn from literature, the Bible, myth or history. Look at the work of U. A. Fanthorpe, Liz Lochhead and Carol Ann Duffy for examples. Such poems can also be inspired by paintings as well as books. *The Poet's View: Poems for Paintings in the Walker Art Gallery*[3] offers many examples. They are made 'dramatic' by having the character speak from a particular moment in their lives. They require empathy, imagination and attention to authentic detail.

Stepping out

Write a poem in the voice or persona (from the Greek for mask) of a figure from history or literature. Think, prior to writing your poem, about how your character would speak; what idiomatic language he/she would use; what colloquialisms. Do research, if necessary, to make yourself familiar with the details of your character's existence, but do not feel you have to put it all in! Let such 'local colour' emerge as and when it seems natural, and your intimacy with your character and their environment will shine through. Try another dramatic monologue based on a character in a painting.

REVISIONS

Most poets find that poems take time to grow, and pass through several drafts before they are finished – sometimes with long pauses in between drafts. Read the poem aloud – you will hear where it flows smoothly or is 'clunking': where it does not work. Do some shaping and pruning, aiming to retain the significant detail, the telling image, and omit superfluous adjectives and adverbs. Then put this draft away for a few days. By leaving it to lie fallow, you will now see more clearly what needs to be done. Revision of a free-form poem usually involves alert tightening of lines, as well as the pruning of language. Sometimes condensing can be achieved by elimination of prosy words and conjunctions, for example, 'and':

then she took the spoon from me and licked it slowly

becoming

> she took the spoon, licked
> it slowly

Your editing might involve radical reshaping and re-arranging of stanzas. While a stanza can be of any length, that length should constitute a kind of paragraphing, each new stanza forwarding the movement of the poem. One line, or even a single word or phrase, can constitute a stanza, but these will need to carry some special importance. Setting a line off by the white space around it draws attention to that line, and this too needs to be justified.

Do not just read, but listen: to poetry on the radio and audio cassettes. Attend poetry readings. Responding to the cadences, language, and rhythms of the poetry you read and hear, your ear will be tuned in, and you will be stimulated for your own work.

ENDING

When is a poem finished? When making your final revisions, the closing lines of your poem, like the beginning, may well be the part that you decide finally to edit out as redundant. You might find that you are over-stating, that what you have wanted to say has already been said or shown. Be careful not to lapse into 'telling', making neat, pat concluding statements when the particulars and imagery of your poem have already achieved the work of sparking your reader's imagination. An awareness of when you are overstating, and your 'sense of an ending' will come with experience. A useful guideline is to remember the power in restraint and understatement.

ADVANCING AS A POET

No one ever became a poet without continually reading poetry, any more than you could become a musician without listening to music. Read omnivorously until you find the poets who excite you. It can be helpful to start with anthologies: historical ones such as the Norton[4] and Oxford[5] anthologies of English verse, and contemporary ones such as *The Rattle Bag*,[6] *The Penguin Book of Contemporary British Poetry*,[7] *The Faber Book of Twentieth-Century Women's Poetry*,[8] or Linda France's *Sixty Women Poets*.[9] Poets talk to each other through their work, and it is through the poems of this month, this year, that the great conversation that is poetry advances. Get hold of the latest issues of poetry magazines, and you will become part of that conversation, if only as a listener at first. Keep reading, keep writing. Poetry is a vocation, and once you follow it you may find that there is no going back.

Notes

1 Lewis Turco, *The New Book of Forms: A Handbook of Poetics* (University Press of New England, Hanover and London, 1986).
2 Sandy Brownjohn, *Does It Have To Rhyme?* (Hodder and Stoughton, London, 1991).
3 *The Poet's View: Poems for Paintings in the Walker Art Gallery*, ed. by Gladys Mary Coles (Headland Press, Wirral, 1996).
4 *The Norton Anthology of Poetry*, ed. by A. W. Allison et al., 3rd edn. (W. W. Norton, New York and London, 1970).
5 *The New Oxford Book of English Verse*, ed. by Helen Gardner (Oxford University Press, Oxford, 1975).
6 *The Rattle Bag*, ed. by Seamus Heaney and Ted Hughes (Faber and Faber, London, 1987).
7 *The Penguin Book of Contemporary British Poetry*, ed. by Andrew Motion and Blake Morrison (Penguin, Harmondsworth, 1993).
8 *The Faber Book of Twentieth-Century Women's Poetry*, ed. by Fleur Adcock (Faber and Faber, London, 1987).
9 Linda France, *Sixty Women Poets* (Bloodaxe, Newcastle-upon-Tyne, 1994).

9 WRITING FOR STAGE

Dymphna Callery

'for the author and then for the actor the word is a small visible portion of a gigantic unseen formation'.

Peter Brook[1]

INTRODUCTION

The stage is a medium of the imagination, conjuring images in the spectators' minds. At the opening of Shakespeare's *Henry V*, the Chorus asks, 'Can this cockpit hold the vasty fields of France?', inviting us to imagine whole battalions of soldiers when we see just one. Language and illusion provoke the spectators' imaginations into seeing what is not there, but what action and words suggest is there. The power of theatre resides in suggestion rather than the imitation of reality: 'the best production takes place in the mind of the beholder'.[2]

The vehicle for drama is not print but flesh and blood: living, breathing actors, moving, still, speaking, silent, in front of our eyes in the present moment. Theatre is a live event, an experience shared between audience and actors.

GETTING STARTED

No one is going to curl up in bed with your play. You are writing for live performance. Playscripts are templates for performance rather than blueprints. Actors, directors and designers bring their particular skills and ideas to interpreting a text, for theatre is a collaborative art. Acknowledging the unique properties of theatre will enable you to exploit its potential and avoid the beginner's problem of writing 'talking heads' where people sit on sofas and explain themselves rather than move around and 'act'. There is little point in writing an unperformable play.

Create a 'theatre of the mind' where you can watch events unfold. Or, better still, see as wide a range of work as you can. It will enhance your awareness of what is possible. Go and sit in an empty theatre and soak up the atmosphere. Try sitting in different places. Ask if you can stand on the stage. This will give you some sense of the nature of the space itself. Try speaking. Imagine the theatre full, the spectators watching your play.

ACTION

Molière declared that all he needed was a couple of planks and a passion. At its simplest the stage is an empty space where anything can happen, and the word 'drama' means action. Imagine an empty stage. Someone enters and finds a letter. They open the letter, read it and tear it into little pieces. They leave. Nothing has been said, yet anyone watching is intrigued. See this happening in your mind's eye. What is in the letter? Who is the person reading it? Decide. Now work out what happens next.

Three different suggestions might be:

- the same person returns and picks up the scraps of paper bar one, and leaves
- another person enters and picks up the scraps and tries to jigsaw them together
- a clown throws the scraps of paper up in the air and pretends it is snowing.

Follow any of these, or your own suggestion, with two further scenes. See how far you can get without using any dialogue, discovering the characters' responses to situations in physical terms: that is, what they *do* rather than worrying about what they say.

David Mamet likens drama to fairy tales, on the basis that we listen to such tales non-judgementally because the characters and situations are presented in only their essential elements. 'The essential task of drama', he says, 'is to offer a solution to a problem which is nonsusceptible to reason ... [to] induce us to suspend our rational judgment, and to follow the *internal* logic of the piece.'[3] So, for example, we suspend our rational judgement with Goldilocks or Cinderella, merely following the order of events.

Write a scenario

Consider what you have written. Try to work out cause and effect, however surreal. To develop the piece, you may introduce a maximum of three performers, and other objects, if you wish, providing people interact with them, but avoid furniture unless you use it in a playful manner (chairs turning into a car, a bed becoming a mountain, for example). The idea is to surprise your spectators whilst retaining an internal logic. Write only the bare essentials; do not describe anything or anyone, simply what happens. Write up to five 'scenes'. This is called a 'scenario' which can be developed further by adding dialogue and creating more events from the situations therein.

It is important to recognize that spectators 'read' visual signals. Every action and gesture on stage is a 'sign', and objects, costume, lighting effects all relay information which spectators will interpret, just as you decided what happened to the letter. Nothing should be on stage without a reason for being there, everything on stage *serves* the action. This applies to words too.

DIALOGUE

Dialogue has three principal functions:

* to embody action
* to move the story on
* to reveal/conceal character.

It is useful to think of speech as 'verbal behaviour', so that it does more than just convey information.[4] At this stage you are training your ear for dialogue without worrying about story, theme or character. Using simple dialogue exercises as starting points can generate ideas for characters and situations. Human beings often reveal more by what they do not say than what they do say, and imply rather than state what they mean.

Yes

Thinking of dialogue as there to intrigue rather than inform, write a scene between two people, A and B, where the only word used is 'Yes' and its variations, e.g. 'Yeah', 'Okay', 'Uh-huh'. Use punctuation, pauses and silence; you may repeat a word within the same line. A maximum of 10 exchanges will do. Ideally, enlist others to read out the result. They will inflect the lines according to both the punctuation and how their partner inflects their lines. You may be surprised that these are not necessarily what you had in mind, but a situation and relationship emerge beneath the 'conversation', perhaps even some sense of character.

However lifelike, dramatic dialogue is not a replica of normal conversation; it is the arrangement of words in an authentically rhythmical pattern which imitates the cadences of everyday speech. This arrangement is designed for maximum dramatic impact, and is essentially a writer's conjuring trick.

Record and condense

Choose a public place, such as a café, or train carriage, where you can listen to people talking at length. Keeping your notebook discreet, write down the dialogue between two strangers you can overhear. Try to record *exactly* what they say, including gaps, repetitions and expletives. At home, read this out and try and work out (a) what their relationship is and (b) what they are talking about. Bearing in mind the previous 'Yes' exercise, write 10 lines of *dramatic* dialogue using this.

    The full conversation has to be condensed, but retain clues as to situation and character. As playwright you work like a translator, who invariably says far less than the original speaker. Try varying and limiting the number of words in any line, say to a maximum of 10, and gauge the effect.

Four paragraphs ago you were invited to write what happens without using speech. Now transpose the action of those scenes into dialogue, using speech as a gloss on what happens. Try to avoid the characters describing the action. So rather than:

A [*tears letter*] I'm going to tear this letter.
You might have:
A [*tears letter*] No!

What your characters say will depend on the scenario that emerged from your 'letter' scenes and the action that arose. Yet the more 'indirect' the dialogue, the more you intrigue your audience. It is also fruitful to notice what is distinctive about the way your characters speak. What are their mannerisms and habits? How do they use grammar or phrasing? Characters in a play must speak consistently, and should be distinguishable by their speech rhythms.

STORY AND PLOT

You do not necessarily start with a whole story. You may start with an idea about characters, situation, fragments of story, or even a few lines of dialogue and develop your play from those. But by practising with a well-known story, you can extend your understanding of the process of playwriting.

    Let us take the story of 'Goldilocks and the Three Bears' and, bearing in mind the previous exercises, write the action and dialogue. Notice the formatting: character names in bold, stage directions in italics, and the different ways of using the pause – one between an exchange, one breaking a line. There is no set method of formatting for plays, but the merit of this method is its clarity.

Scene 1

Three Bears *sit down to breakfast. The porridge is steaming.*
Small Bear	Ow!
Medium Bear	He's burnt his mouth.
Big Bear	We'll go for a walk till it's cool.

They go.

Scene 2

Goldilocks *enters. She tastes the porridge in each bowl, finally eating all in the small bowl.*
Goldilocks	Too hot! Yuk. Too sweet. Cor! Yum. Yum.

She tries each chair and settles on the smallest one. It breaks.
Goldilocks	Ow!

She yawns.
She tests each bed and lies on the smallest one. She falls asleep.

Scene 3

The **Three Bears** *enter.*
Big Bear	Someone's been eating my porridge!
Medium Bear	Someone's been eating my porridge!
Small Bear	Mine's all gone!
Big Bear	Someone's been sitting in my chair!
Medium Bear	Someone's been sitting in my chair!
Small Bear	Mine's all broken.
Big Bear	Someone's been lying on my bed.
Medium Bear	Someone's been lying on my bed.
Small Bear	Look!

Goldilocks *wakes.*
Goldilocks	Aaaahhh!
Big Bear	Grab her!
Medium Bear	Missed!
Small Bear	Come back. Come back!

They chase her from the house.

The story is embodied in the actions, reactions and interactions of the characters in that situation. Story is essentially *character* plus *situation*.

Consider the plot as an obstacle course designed to make a character's journey more engaging and even difficult. The twists and turns of plot arise from your making it hard for characters to get what they want. Macbeth, for example, decides he wants to be king. Duncan is his first obstacle. What if he kills him? Having removed him, King Macbeth sees

Banquo as the obstacle to being 'safely thus', asks 'What if ...?', then removes him. Every time he removes an obstacle another one takes its place.

Dramatize a fairy story

Take a simple fairy tale and dramatize it as we did with Goldilocks. Add substance to it by asking questions and letting your imagination supply possible answers. Try modernizing the story by asking questions with a contemporary ring: in the case of Goldilocks, for example, what if she searched for salt and found a cache of drugs? What if the porridge was spiked? They will lead you on, allowing a topical plot to develop organically whilst still preserving the functions of the characters and situation. What you need to seek is *conflict*, the linchpin of a good plot.

It is dangerous to view conflict as merely loggerhead argument. That way lie the dreaded talking heads. Conflict can exist between character and authority, character and society, character and institution, and it can be embedded within characters as well as surfacing between them. The obvious example is *Hamlet*, where the whole play grows from the protagonist's internal conflict as to whether or not to avenge his father.

THEME

The story of a play might be what happens on the surface but it is not what your play is really about. This is where the stage play often differs from the screenplay, which tends to be driven by narrative. *Waiting for Godot*, for example, is not simply a story of two tramps waiting for someone who never appears. Its theme is existential angst. In *Macbeth*, Shakespeare probes the source and impact of ambition. In *The Cherry Orchard*, Chekhov presents variations on the theme of unrequited love.

When drama deals with the struggles of individuals caught up in big events, it focuses on the universal human subject. Brecht places Mother Courage and her cart against the backdrop of the Thirty Years War: the history of that particular conflict is not as important as the way war reduces human relationships to the fiscal. The theme, in this case, shapes and sustains the momentum.

To some extent a play is the exploration of a problem which is often social or ethical. This is reasonably straightforward if you choose to write about an issue, and there are many worthy examples of 'issue' plays which present a social problem in dramatic form. The idea of using drama to proselytize has been around for centuries. The Church used dramatic reconstructions of biblical stories to reach an illiterate audience in the Middle Ages. The Suffragettes mounted plays which espoused their cause to attract audiences to their meetings. Post-war British theatre abounds with cleverly argued dramas promoting socialism, feminism, anti-racism, gay rights, sympathy for the plight of HIV-positive victims. All of these testify to drama's potential as polemic. Many have been extremely successful in raising consciousness about issues of social and cultural concern. In such plays characters represent specific attitudes towards an issue; the resulting conflict is usually resolved in a way that encourages the audience to side with the underdog.

When characters represent political positions they tend towards stereotype or caricature, depending on the degree of satire. Pillorying attitudes you do not agree with can be great fun, and there is therapeutic delight in controlling characters who represent attitudes you deplore and ensuring they get their come-uppance. Act 1 of Caryl Churchill's *Cloud Nine*, for example, presents a highly effective satire of Victorian imperialism and patriarchal ideology. But what distinguishes this play from other issue plays is the way Churchill exploits the imaginative possibilities of theatre: when the Victorian characters reappear in act 2, set in the 1970s, they have aged only 25 years, and attempt to work out the dysfunctional relationships they have inherited from the past. Although the first act presents an array of stereotypes, the second act reinvents them as unique individuals with contradictions struggling to make sense of their world.

When you read a play, always try and work out what the theme is and sum it up as simply as possible: for example 'love vs. duty', or 'blood is thicker than water'. When you come to write a play, decide what theme it will explore and keep that in mind.

What if ...?

Take a simple newspaper item – tabloids are useful for this – and dramatize it by writing the action and dialogue. Expand the plot by asking 'What if ...?' and following up the ideas in terms of the theme. Ask what attitudes the characters represent in relation to the theme. In other words, what matters to them? This is where you start asking questions of them in order to move the piece beyond a scenario.

CHARACTER

Characters are revealed by the way they respond to situations and events through action, reaction and interaction. Speech is a component, but is the tip of an iceberg. The real business goes on beneath the surface. An audience wants to work out why characters do what they do. Leaving room for them to 'guess' keeps them involved.

If you already know everything about them your play will be lifeless. The trick is to let the characters tell you what is happening, to let them reveal themselves gradually. In writing for the stage, you research your characters while you are writing them.[5] The 'Yes' exercise below gives you some idea of how characters can emerge through the process of writing simple dialogue. Knowing a character's attitude in relation to a chosen theme means you can begin to provoke conflict and tension.

Attitude

Assign A and B oppositional attitudes towards the theme of your piece. Start with a few lines of dialogue between them, using only variants of simple words like 'Yes', with punctuation and pauses as before, but keeping each character's attitude uppermost in your mind. Now let the dialogue continue, using words for a few exchanges. Try to incorporate the advice in the section on dialogue so that you keep it focused.

In the following example, the theme is 'love vs. duty' and the characters are siblings caught in the dilemma of who is to care for their father. The resulting dialogue might run thus:

A	Yes?
B	Okay.
A	You agree?
B	I said okay.
A	Meaning?
B	I'll do my share.
A	Do you love him?
B	Of course.
A	It's not a question of having to.
B	He's my father.

Gradually you get an idea of each character's position and what they want.

Like action and words, characters must serve the play. You need to allow them time to develop, to ferment. 'Writing a play is a quest',[6] states Sheila Yeger, and in the early stages you are finding out who the characters are and what your play is about.

Remember also that in art, as in life, human beings are flawed, vulnerable and deceitful, even when they are heroic! Humans are full of contradictions, which is what makes them unique and interesting. If you give the best lines to the villain, your play will be the richer.

Although you want to create characters with individual traits, it is more important to ask questions of them than accumulate details. An actor cannot play shoe-size. Hot-seating is a game that encourages you to discover more about your characters.

The hot-seat

Each playwright takes a turn in the 'hot-seat' and the others fire questions at them, such as 'What do you vote?' or 'What is your favourite book/TV programme/film?' and the 'hot-seater' replies on behalf of one of the characters in their play. Avoid questions about personal habits and physical appearance, and focus instead on characters' attitudes. You need to know what matters to them. Ask and respond quickly – one minute per playwright.

You may be surprised by your answers! But such spontaneity can offer a direct line to a character's impulses. In real life we act and speak spontaneously. To be credible, characters must appear to do so. Peter Brook tells his actors that 'a word does not begin as a word, it begins as an impulse'.[7] The same applies to actions.

SPEECHES

Writing monologues for your characters is an excellent way of getting 'inside' them. Characters may off-load what is in their mind, sharing their thoughts with other characters, or alone with the audience. They may comment on the action, offer their opinion, state their case, or even explode into an aria of expression. Lucky's long speech in the middle of *Waiting for Godot* is an extraordinary outburst which encapsulates the despair of language ever holding meaning.

Characters share their thoughts in a 'private' or 'public' manner, depending on the style of play. The former is a soliloquy, or spoken thought process, and the character may or may not acknowledge the audience. The latter is where characters acknowledge the presence of the audience openly, in the manner of 'stand-up', and is more common in issue plays.

Take one of the 'characters' you have been working with so far. Pinpoint a moment in one of the exercises where they are under pressure and write a speech expressing what they feel. Experiment with writing private and public versions.

SUBTEXT

What characters want is termed motivation. This is what drives them, their conscious and unconscious desires, so that each character has their own agenda. More often than not such agendas are hidden. They emerge when a character is put under pressure. But characters also pursue their desires by devious means, intentionally and unintentionally. An audience wants 'to find out who wants what from whom'.[8] This is where motivation links with subtext.

At its simplest, subtext is what characters feel/think/want but do not say. The art of playwriting is to some extent the mastery of subtext: setting up conflicting desires without stating them.

What they want

Write a scene between your two characters where one gets what they want without stating it. Make sure you know where we are and what the situation is. Use any of the characters and situations which have emerged in the exercises so far.

Following on from the earlier exercise with A and B: Alice is preparing to bury father in the garden and wants her brother Bob's help:

Alice *digs.* **Bob** *watches.*
Bob   We can't bury him here. It's illegal.
Alice   When did he ever care about legality?
Bob   You'll get caught.
Alice   Not if you don't tell.
Pause.
Bob   This is a garden. It's not consecrated ground.
Alice   He was an atheist. [*Pause.*] I'm only doing what he wanted, Bob.
Bob   Where's the other shovel?

Notice how the power shifts between the characters as though, as in a tennis match, the exchanges become a rally with points being scored.

All human interaction functions in terms of status. It is the see-saw principle upon which the power shifts in relationships. Assigning status is a useful way of differentiating your characters and 'the gap between assumed and assigned status is a rich source of conflict'.[9] A classic status relationship is that of master/servant. A more subtle illustration of a relationship founded on mutual dependence can be found between Vladimir and Estragon in *Waiting for Godot*.

You can observe status by watching your friends and assigning them status numbers: 1 = someone who plays low, 10 = someone who plays high, and degrees in between. Once you have grasped the principle, try assigning your characters status numbers. You can play with status by either maintaining their number, or by getting low to 'play' high and vice versa. Comedy often operates on this principle with, for example, a servant playing high status when the master is not looking.

Changing status

Consider your own version of the subtext exercise. Who has the higher status at the beginning? And who is higher at the end of the scene? Experiment with exaggerating the status shifts either by speech or action in a new draft: the aim is to 'up the stakes' at each point.

A heightened version of the previous scene might run:

Alice *digs furiously.* **Bob** *watches.*
Bob   You can't bury him here. It's illegal.
Alice   Illegal ! Since when did you care about legality?
Bob   You'll go to prison.
Alice   Only if you tell.
Bob *kicks the ground.*
Bob   This is an allotment, for god's sake. It's not even consecrated ground.
Alice   He was an atheist. [*She rests on her spade.*] I'm only doing what he wanted, Bob.
Bob   All right then. Where's the other shovel?

The amendments are slight but the see-saw is more obvious. It does not necessarily make a better script, but it reveals more about the undercurrents in this relationship. The scene is also moving closer to comedy, partly because the choice of 'allotment' rather than 'garden' is more absurd, partly because the characters seem more like bickering siblings.

Notice how the plot is beginning to develop. We have two major scenes, one before the father's death from an earlier exercise, and one after. Asking 'What if someone finds out?' can provoke a final outcome. For instance, Alice be might prosecuted for breaking the law, with Bob committing perjury by stating he knew nothing of the illegal burial.

STRUCTURING THE WHOLE

Now you have several short scenes and a monologue. If these are connected thematically you might have the beginnings of a play, especially if you have an ending in mind. Endings are like punchlines, both inevitable and surprising. They also present a kind of summing up of the play. At the ends of *Hamlet* and *Macbeth*, carnage is accompanied by insight. Beckett's two tramps talk of going but stay. Brecht's Mother Courage still pulls her cart across Europe. Alice and Bob replay sibling rivalry in public. Knowing the ending means that you can work towards it.

Mapping

Take a group of scenes from any of the previous exercises, either an adaptation of a fairy tale, or the 'letter' exercise, or the newspaper item, and decide on an ending for the story. Now work out what needs to happen to lead to that point. Do not write any more just yet. At this point you are merely creating the map of what happens before deciding how to organize the journey of the play.

Reading plays is helpful. You discover how playwrights organize their material to create dramatic effects. Sometimes plays are organized in a manner which allows several stories to be connected by theme, rather than fitting into one overarching narrative like Hollywood movies. Some of the most vibrant modern plays utilize non-linear structures where the onus on interpreting narrative(s) and meaning(s) is on the spectator. Yet the best plays still offer an audience a coherent experience. *Waiting for Godot* has a perfectly balanced two-part structure which works like counterpoint and suits the tragicomic nature of the play. Charlotte Keatley's *My Mother Said I Never Should* combines naturalistic scenes of four generations of women with surreal scenes between the characters as children. The dreamlike structure brings it closer to the landscape of memory than the map of history without losing the sense of mounting tension, climax and resolution normally ascribed to classic narrative structure.

It is the way in which you assemble the elements of your play that gives it coherence. You may choose to make your theme clear by juxtaposition and contrast, or follow the story of a protagonist, or present a collage poem in the manner of Ntozake Shange's *For Colored Girls Who Have Considered Suicide When The Rainbow Is Enuf*. Whatever your choice of structure, the purpose is to take your audience on a journey, and here the Aristotelian elements of conflict, mounting tension and resolution (or at least restoring order to chaos) provide a valuable model.

Having decided what kind of structure you are using, you need to break down the journey of the play into sections. Plays are made up of scenes, each one a unit which either introduces a new idea or develops those of previous scenes in a new location or different time. Each scene moves us on to another episode, yet each one operates like a mini-play embodying conflict, tension and moving *towards* a resolution, which may be the source of further conflict.

Divide and rule

Go back to the previous exercise, and divide the 'map' you have devised into scenes. It is a good idea to give them titles as well as numbers, so, for example, 'Alice appears in court' might be the title of the next part of our illegal burial story.

Every scene needs a purpose or *objective* in relation to the whole. Once your theme and characters start to emerge and you have a map of the whole play in your head, you can assign objectives to each scene. You now know what each character wants *in each scene* and which part of the story happens in *each scene*. It is like putting a jigsaw together with pieces of varying size and shape. Remember that varying the length of scenes will create a more interesting rhythmic pattern for the whole.

Assign objectives to each scene. Now write each scene with that objective in mind. Start them as late as possible, and finish them as early, as though you move in on people deep in conversation and leave before they have finished. Bear in mind also that there needs to be some degree of urgency in order to create tension.

'Putting a clock on a scene' is an excellent method for injecting tension. Take one of the scenes you have written and revise it on the basis that either (a) someone else is due to arrive, or (b) one character has another pressing engagement. Try to avoid phrases like 'I have to go', or 'so-and-so is coming'.

Now you are beginning to write the first draft of a play. This will necessarily go through several drafts and be edited and redrafted if it gets into rehearsal. Getting drama students to read out your work will also teach you what 'works', whether a line 'rings true' or not, where the rhythm is awkward, when boredom sets in. Inevitably you will get it wrong! That is how you learn.

CONCLUSION

The best way to make progress is to observe how other dramatists do it. Watching and reading plays extends your knowledge of the medium and the plays referred to in this chapter are suggestions for reading. Better still, if you have an opportunity to watch rehearsals or drama workshops, or attend a local youth theatre or student drama group, then take it. Gaining experience of what happens in the theatre-making process will provide insights you can exploit. Playwriting is a process of trial and error, but ultimately the action and words need to work in that extraordinary three-dimensional empty space we call the theatre.

Notes

1 Peter Brook, *The Empty Space* (Methuen, London, 1968).
2 David Mamet, *A Whore's Profession* (Faber, London, 1994).
3 Mamet, *A Whore's Profession*.

4 Paul Mills, *Writing in Action* (Routledge, London, 1996).
5 Mills, *Writing in Action*.
6 Sheila Yeger, *The Sound of One Hand Clapping: A Guide to Writing for the Theatre* (Amber Lane Press, Oxford, 1990).
7 Brook, *The Empty Space*.
8 Mills, *Writing in Action*.
9 Yeger, *The Sound of One Hand Clapping*.

10 WRITING FOR RADIO

Aileen La Tourette

'The voice is a second face.'[1]

INTRODUCTION

Radio is a wonderful medium for a writer. There are no restrictions on your imagination. You can move time around at will, create separate worlds, play whatever tricks you like to get your meaning across. The dead can speak, the inanimate can come to life. All you have to do is cue your listeners so that they can imagine with you. You are issuing an invitation to them to come with you into another world. It may be familiar or unfamiliar, contemporary or historical, realistic or bizarre. It can be whatever you want it to be, provided you can bring it to life inside the listeners' heads. Radio is imagination speaking to imagination in a very direct way. It is a very intimate form of expression and communication and a very satisfying one for a writer.

On a practical level, it is far cheaper to 'stage' a radio drama in a studio than to shoot a film or mount a production in a theatre. Your work has arguably more chance of being heard than it has of being seen, especially if you explore some of the possibilities of local radio discussed at the end of the chapter.

GETTING STARTED

If you want to write for radio – to write radio drama, perhaps, or adapt a classic book for radio – the first thing you have to do is listen. If you are drawn to radio as a medium, chances are you already are a good listener. You need to become an even better one. Sound is what radio is about, even more than words.

Listen up

If you live in a city, listen with your eyes closed to what makes a city, in an audio sense. What do you hear from the top of a bus, in the underground, on the street? If you live in the country, what do you hear, and where? Try listening at different times of the day and night. How do the sounds change? Now try the same exercise in different interior spaces. What sounds create the atmosphere of an office, a classroom, a library, a church? Are there different 'sounds of silence'? If so, how are they different?

Learning the medium

Develop the habit of listening to radio. Turn it on at odd moments and get a feel for which programmes are broadcast at different hours of the day and night, how long they last and who they are aimed at. You need to know the ins and outs of your medium. Listen to radio drama, to the classic serial. Read radio previews and reviews in the press. Buy the *Radio Times* and see how radio plays are described. Which ones make you want to listen? Later on in the chapter, you will be asked to write a synopsis of your play.

STARTING YOUR PLAY: MONOLOGUE

Monologue is a good way to begin your radio writing. In a monologue, one person is speaking, often to themselves. The monologue may include other voices, echoes in the main character's memory, or fantasies in which the character imagines the future. Radio lets you into the characters' heads. Think of Alan Bennett's *Talking Heads*, a series of monologues that worked brilliantly on TV and was equally effective when simply listened to. A character engaged in monologue talks freely. They may reveal things that are usually kept secret. You may have a character watering plants and chattering away, or walking a dog and talking aloud, or wheeling a sleeping baby in a pram and telling it things that cannot be revealed to anyone else, to anyone who would really understand. Remember to contextualize your monologue, in other words to find a way, such as the pram or the dog-walking, to make it plausible that your character would be talking to themselves at this moment in time. They might be drunk, or trying not to fall asleep behind the wheel of a car. You may object, quite rightly, that the monologues of *Talking Heads* are not contextualized, nor are Spalding Gray's monologues,[2] another example you should have a look at. They simply start off, making the monologue its own context. All rules are made to be broken, but you need to serve an apprenticeship first, and show that you know what the rules are, and how they work.

The morning after

Does a room sound different when there has been an argument in it? When there has been a party in it? How would a character in a radio play express the feeling of a 'morning-after' party room, or bedroom? Imagine the words he or she would use, the sounds they might make clearing up, making the bed. Imagine what might be going on in their minds. Now write a brief morning-after speech for such a character. They might say it aloud, or in the echoey tone that tells you a character is thinking the speech, saying it inside their own heads. This is indicated in a script by the words *To us*, or *VO* for *voice-over*.

Try your morning-after monologue both as voice-over, from inside the character's head, and as a speech delivered aloud. Have someone read it at first without any direction from you. Can they make sense of it without long explanations? If not, you may have left too much of it in your own head, and not delivered it onto the page. You know what you are trying to say, your actor does not, unless you tell them clearly. Do not assume that any lack of understanding is their fault. It may be yours. When you think the monologue is right, have them read it again. Now direct them, telling them how to get the emphasis you intend for the character they are playing. When you are satisfied with their performance, record the monologue and listen to it. Remember to time it as well. You should time every radio piece you ever write, to get into the habit of noticing how long your work takes.

The morning after, part 2

Now imagine that another character has overheard this monologue, which your character has, perhaps unconsciously, spoken out loud. How will the second character react? Will they make their presence known, or not? You now have the beginnings of a plot, and the first glimmerings of character. You have also begun using dialogue, which we will come back to.

Shopping around

Have a look at Chapter 1, 'Observation and discovery', to hone your investigative skills. Pick a character from a queue at a supermarket checkout. Try and imagine what might be in your character's mind from the purchases in their basket. Do they live alone, are they responsible for a family, have they included luxury items or strictly necessary ones? Imagine how they feel about the products in their shopping cart. Do they feel deprived or privileged, are they looking forward to going home and unloading, or dreading the next step of cooking a meal? Fill out your monologue with information about where and how they live.

Now try to get inside the head of the woman or man behind the checkout counter. How long have they been there, today or forever? What do they think of the customers, of their choices? Try to avoid cliché. Maybe the person at the checkout is thrilled to have their job, maybe they see it as an escape from boredom and tedium and poverty. Do not make assumptions, make observations. Imagine hearing the bleeps of the machine that reads the bar codes and the ring of the till all day long. Maybe the person at the checkout is saving up for something. What?

You can repeat this exercise in bus and post office queues, doctors' and dentists' waiting rooms. Set up the scene in your head by establishing the background noises which deliver the atmosphere, so that the listener will know immediately where they are (unless you want to keep them in suspense for a time). Notice that these exercises are about both setting and character. People behave in particular ways in particular places and situations, at the dentist's, for instance. Some people will react nervously, others show bravado. Some may be loud and complain a lot. Some people at the checkout will be polite and friendly, some not.

When you have written a monologue that you especially like, have someone act it and listen to the result. Record it, noting how long it is – that its, how much time it takes, not how many pages. You may be surprised how short your work is, once it is spoken.

Now imagine what might have come before the monologue and what might come after it. With your actor, improvise these scenes. You will find yourselves using dialogue, of course. That means simply speaking to each other, having an exchange.

DIALOGUE

Think about dialogue in the widest sense, as involving sound as well as words. There is a dialogue of wood and saw, a dialogue of vegetable board and chopper. How a character saws wood, or chops vegetables, will tell you a lot about their mood. It might be far more effective to begin a scene with a loud, furious or frantic chopping of vegetables than with someone saying how angry they are, or how nervous they are about preparing dinner for their boss. Or you could begin the first scene with a slammed door. Is someone leaving, is there a big storm brewing outside, or both? Any sound effect which sets up questions in the listeners' minds is a good start for a radio play. Music can also be highly useful in establishing a mood. Music is another form of dialogue which works extremely well on radio.

People in plays – or books, for that matter – do not speak exactly like people in real life. The dialogue you need to write is more allusive, more subtle. You need to prune the boringness and repetition from speech in order for it to work in a play, unless you are using these attributes – boringness and repetitiveness – as a feature, perhaps for humour. Even if you are, your dialogue will be structured. It will not be like the dialogue in real life, or not exactly like it. Your listening skills will come in handy – learn to glean the essence of a conversation and deliver it in tight, quick form. That is what developing an ear for dialogue really means.

Learn to hear not only what people say but the way they say it. There are many different ways of saying the simplest things, like 'hello'. The word may be the same, but how different it sounds in the mouths of lovers, of strangers, of people reunited after years of separation! These are only a few examples. Think of the simplest everyday exchanges, the 'How are you'/ 'I'm fine' exchanges we all experience constantly, and what they say about us, or fail to say.

Greetings and farewells

Improvise this exercise with friends, perhaps with a local drama group. Act out as many hellos and goodbyes as you can imagine. You may be frostily polite, or warmly passionate. You may be greeting your partner or long-lost parent, son or daughter. You may be saying goodbye from the deck of a ship, or from the threshold of a room. Try and think yourselves into these situations and see what dialogue emerges. Keep it brief. Never pad unless this is what your characters are doing, to cover up a tense moment.

INDIRECT DIALOGUE

Develop an ear for what people do not say, for what remains unspoken. Your dialogue will need to suggest what characters feel and do not say, as well as carry meanings the characters might not intend, or might be trying to avoid. These elements are part of what we call indirect dialogue, defined by Martin Esslin as: 'the characters' oblique reference to the subject under discussion, since they cannot find the courage to display their feelings openly'.[3] Esslin also says: 'Chekov used indirect dialogue in situations when their characters are too shy to express their real thoughts and hide their emotions behind trivial subjects.'⁴ Think of the way people talk about the weather. Are they sometimes really talking about something else, something to do with the way they feel? If it is a sunny day and someone shivers and says yes but it is too cold, could they be talking about their own inner state as well as the outer one? People find all kinds of ingenious ways of talking about things – or not talking about them. For example, suppose a mother is waiting at home for her son to arrive. She has had a phone call that day from the school, informing her that he has not turned up for the past two weeks. He comes in at the usual time, as he always does, pretending nothing is wrong. She goes along with it:

Heavy rain, thunder and lightning. Outer door slams. Sound of someone running upstairs.

Gerry [*shouts*] Mum?
Mum I'm in the kitchen. [*To us.*] Why does he always shout?
Gerry comes in, dripping wet
Mum I just washed that floor.
Gerry Cleaner now, innit? Any biscuits about?
Mum You know where they are if there are. Did you walk home alone?
Gerry Yeah. No. With Paul.
Mum Paul who?
Gerry You know. Paul.
Mum The older boy.
Gerry [*Mouth full of biscuit*] Bit oldern me. Yeah.
Mum Likes to walk in the rain, does he?
Gerry Ain't got a lot of choice today.
Mum Choice. Now there's an interesting word.
Gerry What's up with you, Mum? You stuck inside all day in the rain or somethink?
Baby starts to cry
Mum As you said, son, I don't have a lot of choice.
She sweeps out of the room
Gerry [*To us*] I hate it when she calls me son. She sounds like she knows – no. She couldn't. [*Shouts.*] Mum, where'd you say the biscuits are?

Note the use of *to us* to indicate that Gerry is speaking inside his head. Note also the spacing and the way the script is laid out. It is important that your work is neat, clear and well presented in any genre, including radio. Stage directions – using words like *Shouts* to tell the actor how to say a line – should be kept to the minimum. Here is another sample of indirect dialogue.

Sound of someone chopping vegetables, very fast and very loud. Prison kitchen background of radio playing sad song, whistling, bit of banter, bubbling pots. Someone comes in.

Officer	You aren't crying, are you? Big boy like you?
Albert	I'm chopping onions.
Officer	Ah. Yes. Onions.
Albert	You want to chop some, Mr Allen?
Officer	Uh, no thanks, Al. You go right ahead and, uh, cry.

He leaves.

| Albert | Tosser. |

Chopping stops.

| Albert | [*To us*] Bet you could chop onions and not cry a tear. Bet you don't know how. Mr He-man. Mr Ex-army. I intend to see that onions are on the menu every day that I work in this kitchen, Mr Allen. [*Crying.*] That way I might stay human, in spite of you. In spite of the nick. In spite of the onions. |

Chopping resumes.

Remember, you must ensure that your characters are distinct from one another. We need to know who is speaking at all times, without confusion. The dialogue must contain tension which builds towards a release or revelation of some kind. The release may come or it may not come; the revelation may be that there is no revelation. It is up to you. The onion man may be taken off kitchen duty and put in the laundry or on some other job detail where he cannot cry. He may complain to himself of feeling all dammed up and he may get into a fight as a result. Or he may be put on garden detail and start planting onions instead of petunias in the prison's front garden, because it makes him feel better.

More indirect dialogue

Write three different dialogues about the weather, or about some other mundane subject like food or drink. In David Mamet's *Duck Variations*, two old men meet in the park and talk about the ducks in the duck pond, but they really talk about many different things through the medium of the ducks. Mamet's dialogues are very funny; see if you can get some humour into yours.

When you have written your dialogues, have two friends act them for you. As with your monologues, give them some director's notes, but also take note, yourself, of what seems unclear in your script, and correct it. When you and the actors are ready, tape the dialogues and listen to them. You may be surprised at what works and what does not. Play the tapes to other people and listen to their reactions.

Direct and indirect dialogue

Write a dialogue between two people in a bank, at a bus stop, in an elevator, in direct dialogue. Now rewrite them in indirect dialogue.

Try a combination of the two – this is what most dialogues turn out to be. Have your actors do the dialogues for you, so you can hear the differences. Sometimes very flat, realistic dialogue can be very funny or, in a time of stress like a bereavement, for example, very sad. Write a direct dialogue between two people picking out flowers at the florist's for a tribute to a dead friend. Write a direct dialogue between two people who are deciding to get a divorce. Now write both in indirect dialogue. The same two people are skirting round the issue of the flowers, and the death; and skirting round the issue of divorce. Perhaps the indirect dialogue might come earlier on in the play, followed by a very sharp, direct exchange which would be all the more poignant for what had gone before. Try your dialogues in sequence like this, starting with the indirect and ending with the direct. Then try them the opposite way round.

STRUCTURE

All drama needs structure. With radio plays in particular, where you are leading the listener blind through the action and dialogue, you will need to develop your plot in a coherent way. You may not wish to structure your play this tightly, but you need to know how structure works. Particularly on radio, where you are leading the listener blind through the action and dialogue, you will need to develop your play in a coherent way.

> A writer must get in touch with the reader by putting before him something which he recognizes, and therefore stimulates his imagination, and makes him willing to co-operate in the far more difficult business of intimacy. And it is of the highest importance that this common meeting-place should be reached easily, almost instinctively, in the dark, with one's eyes shut.[5]

Here Virginia Woolf is talking about writing on the page. But what she says applies to radio, where you are stimulating your listeners' imaginations and inviting them to participate in the peculiar intimacy of the medium. To make the listener feel safe – not too safe, but safe enough to venture into imaginative space with you – structure is necessary. It strengthens and clarifies your play. All plays need a protagonist – a central character – and an antagonist, who causes the main character some kind of conflict. Conflict is the core of drama. Actors are told to think in terms of verbs, not adjectives – in other words, to define characters by what they do, or want to do. That word 'want' is very important. According to the great director and theoretician Stanislavski, desire is the essence of theatre. Desire is what moves characters to action. Think of

Macbeth and the way the three witches taunt him and play on his ambition. Read, or re-read, *Macbeth,* and see if you can get hold of a tape of a radio performance of the play. The famous sleepwalking scene where guilt makes Lady Macbeth wash her hands over and over plays to great effect, and Banquo's ghost can also be performed with maximum effectiveness on radio. Listeners can imagine the ghost for themselves; they only need Shakespeare's words. What you hear in *Macbeth* is what all plays must include: some kind of setting-up or establishing scene, some kind of disturbance leading to a climax, and some kind of resolution. Now get hold of a copy of a contemporary play, and a tape if possible, for example of Charlotte Keatley's *My Mother Said I Never Should,* performed both in the theatre and on radio. What do the characters want – do they know? Do they deceive themselves, like Macbeth? How honest are they with each other, and what do their lies – to themselves and others – reveal about them? Your characters cannot always be nice, or they will not be real.

Go for it

You may want to attempt a three-act play according to the structure laid out in Chapter 9, 'Writing for stage'. You may think of a plot which can observe the Aristotelian unities of time, space and action. Your play will happen in a single day, in a single setting, and the action of the play will dramatize one central story. But even Aristotle would probably have been tempted to use flashback, if there had been radio in his time!

Imagine that your protagonist has died. Your play is set on the day of the funeral. It takes place in the home of the deceased, after the actual service has taken place. People are eating and drinking and revealing information constantly. There are flashbacks to the funeral service, and to times when the deceased was alive. Start with the subdued hubbub of the post-funeral gathering, people talking quietly and respectfully. The deceased could be a young rock star who died of a drug overdose, or a young woman on a council estate who died of anorexia. Either character would have a whole cast of mourners. Perhaps the rock star had more than one partner. Perhaps they did not know about each other, which could lead to conflict, and to humour. Perhaps the anorexic woman had a crush on another woman which she was terrified to reveal. Perhaps the deceased is a female rock star, or a male anorexic. The real hero or heroine of the play is the dead person around whom, in a sense, all the action revolves. You will almost certainly flash back – probably in act 2 – to the character's youth, to try and put their life in perspective and uncover an incident which might help explain the way they died. Try not to explain them too neatly. Then the last act would probably return to the wake. We would hear what the nearest and dearest of the late character said with much more understanding, because of the flashback. You might want to make the dead person a character at his or her own wake, responding to comments in voice-over. At the end of the play you might discover that the wake and the funeral were fantasies, and the character is still alive. Or you might not. Tricks might sound good in theory, but they are hard to bring off successfully.

DRAFTING

When you have a draft of a play that feels as right as you can get it, try it with actors. If you have worked with the same actors during the preceding exercises, you may be lucky enough to have built up a relationship with people who know your work. Listen to it, and redraft the play on the basis of what you hear. Sometimes cherished lines and speeches have to go. They simply do not work, whereas other bits, lines you are not particularly proud of, will work brilliantly. It is up to you to develop an ear for your own work, and to be ruthlessly honest with yourself when you listen to it. Refer to the chapter on editing to help you with this process.

Listen to the play again, and redraft it if necessary. When you are ready, direct it, and record it. Listen hard and learn where its weaknesses and strengths are. You will find it a thrilling process to have live actors saying your lines, and you will find that the lines change when they are spoken outside your own head. You may need to write another draft of your play after hearing the tape, or you may decide to move on to something else. Remember your timing. If your play is three hours long, it is unlikely to be broadcast.

MARKETING YOUR PLAY

Selling a radio play will take persistence. First of all, explore local possibilities. Find out whether there are any radio slots for beginners offered by local stations, as there are, for example, in Merseyside. See if you can get a local station to let you into a studio to play around with sound effects and explore the possibilities of the medium. Try hospital radio, which might welcome a short drama for patients to listen to, or even a soap. Try any and all local radio stations. Even if you do not actually sell a radio idea or a finished play, you will make valuable contacts and receive valuable advice.

THE SYNOPSIS

Try contacting local stations by phone first. If you are encouraged to send in a play or a synopsis, think hard about how to sell your idea. Fashions in synopsis writing change as markets change. BBC Radio Drama currently quite like an introductory sentence or two saying how the idea for the play came to you.

If you are sending in a play and a synopsis – and you should always include a synopsis with any playscript you submit – to the BBC or to any radio station, remember that they receive many submissions. It will take them time to read your script. Try to be patient. Your script will be read faster by a local station than by the BBC, who receive hundreds of scripts per month.

This is a time for your belief in your work, and your confidence in yourself, to come to the fore. Never apologize for any aspect of your work. Also remember that confidence is not the same thing as arrogance. You are proud of what you have written, and confident because it has gone through a long process of drafting and redrafting, of thought and improvisation and polishing. You are confident because of the process of writing itself. If you have followed all the steps, and not been self-indulgent about hanging on to favourite lines even when you can hear that they do not work, you are ready to summarize your work in a brief, positive way:

Synopsis of *Nursing Ambition* (a 50-minute play for radio)
Every little girl wants to be a nurse at some time or other. I certainly did, and I read about nurses in series of books that made them seem glamorous and heroic – a hard combination to beat.

Sarah, the central character of *Nursing Ambition,* is a nurse, and she is having a disillusioning time of it. She, too, remembers the books about nurses she read as a child. The play opens with one such extract, exaggerated for comic effect: 'Marsha knew the profession of nursing was a noble calling. She thought of Florence Nightingale, that brave, wonderful lady with the lamp. Could she ever be worthy to follow in her footsteps?'

As the play goes on, Sarah is haunted by the ghost of Florence Nightingale, the real Florence Nightingale, who turns out to be at least as thoroughly disillusioned with the system as Sarah herself. The comic dialogue between the two grouchy, exhausted nurses illustrates exactly what an underrated profession nursing has always been – in a humorous way.

You would then go on to outline the rest of the plot, with examples of dialogue that give a flavour of the characters and of the play. You would say where it was set. You would have researched the slots available, of course, and timed the play to fit into one of them.

You have done everything you could to make your play work. Now it is up to forces beyond your control. Give yourself a rest. You may find your next idea starts to brew. Start making notes as you would for any piece of work – and so the process continues. Good luck and good listening.

Notes

1 Gerard Bower, *Carnets*, quoted in *The Oxford Book of Quotations* (Oxford University Press, Oxford, 1992).
2 Spalding Gray, *Swimming to Cambodia* (Theatre Communications Group, New York, 1999).
3 Martin Esslin, *The Theatre of the Absurd* (Penguin Books, London, 1991).
4 Esslin, *Theatre of the Absurd*.
5 Virginia Woolf, 'Mr. Bennett and Mrs. Brown', in *The Captain's Death Bed and Other Essays* (Hogarth Press, London, 1950).

11 WRITING A NOVEL

James Friel

GETTING STARTED AND KEEPING GOING

In a novel you are free to describe, to narrate, to joke, to teach. You can move a reader to laughter, tears, outrage or contemplation. You are free to invent, to record the world, remember the past, to reshape your own experience and to mimic the thoughts of others. You are allowed to tell any number of small lies and quite a few large ones in the hope of revealing more significant truths. You can take on the world, fight wars, travel in time, explore new planets or confine yourself to one character, one room, one day.

The novel allows you to do all this and more – and to do so at length.

Such freedom comes at a price. Time. Novels take time, lots of it. It is a price worth paying.

Inspiration is powerful but short-lived. The idea for a novel can come like a pentecostal flame. It can take over your whole being. It can drive you to start but will not sustain you through the long age it can take to complete one. No novel was ever written in an afternoon.

You may have this time and waste it. More often, you do not. Money, work, family, friends, sickness, the desire for leisure all make demands upon our time: life, for a writer, is that which interrupts. You must make time, steal time, use it. You must learn to acquire discipline – the habit of work – to carve out a slice of time in which your novel gets written.

* Set aside a time – ideally every day – when you write. Although it is difficult, try and keep to it. Family and friends may interrupt – they may even mock at first – but most people will come to respect your routine. More importantly, you will come to need this time and to insist on it.
* Keep to this time even if no writing is achieved. It may be dispiriting to sit and fail to produce anything worthwhile but, by keeping the

appointment, you are developing a muscle that will help you later on.

- Do not make the situation in which you can work – the house must be empty, the paper must be yellow and unlined, the ink must be blue – too demanding. It will become a means to prevaricate, a way of *not* writing.

- Minimize distractions. Music, pleasant views, interesting books may create an atmosphere and may, initially, stimulate but in time they might distract you. If you must have something, have a board pinned with images relevant to your novel. Don De Lillo keeps a picture of a stern-looking Jorge Luis Borges in front of him – 'a writer who did not waste time at the window or anywhere else'.[1]

- Franz Kafka wrote that a writer's sanity is dependent on his desk: if you want to escape madness, you should not leave your desk but cling to it with your teeth. This may be considered a little extreme. Even the most rigorous of us will slip. Reward good behaviour. Punish bad. Develop a conscience.

DRAFTING A NOVEL

Do not deny yourself the pleasure of planning and dreaming your novel. Iris Murdoch said this was the best part of writing and claimed to have pondered everything that was going to happen before she set pen to paper. This meant she could concentrate not on *what* she was going to write but *how*.

Some writers plan very little. They need to feel the white heat of writing and inventing at the same time. Others, like Anthony Burgess, make a few short notes about the story's beginning, middle and end and then draft the first page, revise it and go on in that way until the novel is completed.

Joyce Cary and Vladimir Nabokov wrote whatever each was moved to write on the day concerned – Nabokov working on index cards and seldom in consecutive order, rewriting each snippet many times and, when complete, sewing them together.

The ways to work at a novel are many but what matters is that your draft will be the result of a habit of writing, the consequence of maintaining the discipline of getting your thoughts down. John Steinbeck would advise you to abandon the idea that you are ever going to finish and instead plan to write a page a day.[2] This is good advice in that it encourages discipline but does not allow you to be overwhelmed by all that you have yet to do.

Trust your work to have its own energy, will, momentum, secrets. It is for this reason alone that it may be best for you to go at your first draft free-fall, free style. Avoid correcting or rewriting until the end of either each chapter or section, or when the whole novel is down in one draft. Feel the flow. Respond to its rhythm. If a scene bogs you down, be patient or move on to another. Perhaps the scene you are struggling with does not belong at all and this is the way it is telling you.

Do not worry overmuch about repetitious words, phrases or images. Until you are deeper into your written world, you may not be able to judge or understand every detail your writing throws up, its import or its necessity. That comes with rewriting when you will hold every word, sentence, image and idea up to the light. Work by intuition. Trust the tale.

Be kind to yourself and to it. A first draft is allowed to fail, to dissatisfy. The idea that your prose should stand immediately to shiny attention is a form of laziness. You are trying to avoid the hard work of training and grooming it, of listening to what works and what does not, of picking it up when it stumbles. It is *allowed* not to be good at a first, second, third or twentieth draft. It does not have to be perfect until it is finished – and not even then.

Be your own critic. Be your own cheerleader. There are days when you will need to be both. You cannot rely on others to tell you when your work is going well. Of course everyone relishes praise and feels the need for feedback but, in the end, you are blunting your own perceptions by replacing them with the opinion of others who may be too biased or too fond to give you the response your work needs.

Far better to be your own editor by using your writer's journal to record your doubts, anxieties and victories as your work evolves. By honest appraisal of your own efforts – by the very act of putting down your thoughts – you may come to solve the problem that is currently occupying you.

STRUCTURE AND PLOTTING

Conventionally, most tales share a basic structure:

- stasis
- a trigger that upsets the stasis
- a quest to recover it
- a surprise development
- a critical choice
- a climax
- a reversal
- and a solution.

Consider well-known stories from *Oedipus* and *Hamlet* to 'Cinderella', *Wind in the Willows* and *Gone with the Wind* and you will find they correspond to this pattern.

STRUCTURING YOUR NOVEL

Consider your own idea for a novel. Does it have classic structures? Sketch out where it fits and where it does not. Ask yourself if a failure to fit the classic structure is a weakness or a strength.

Remember that, whether or not your idea matches that classic structure, it will also have its own shape, integrity, coherence. D. H. Lawrence said that: 'all the rules of construction hold good only for novels that are copies of other novels. A book which is not a copy of other books has its own construction.'[3]

You may have an idea for a novel already. If so, find its construction by thinking of shape, echoes and balances, and fostering your pattern-making intelligence. (Fostering, not *developing*, because you have that intelligence already. That is implicit in your desire to represent life in novel shape.)

Structure is not some terrible obstacle to be overcome. It is you deciding how your story is to be told. As an example, here is a plan in 15 points, based on a fictional series of newspaper headings and articles:

1. LINA LAMONT DEAD: MOVIE STAR MURDERED
   HUSBAND ARRESTED THREE HOURS LATER IN CHINATOWN
   OPIUM DEN
   Former Silent Movie Queen Murdered On Eve Of Comeback.
   Shot To Death In Bedroom.

2. Dead Star Had Bullet Wounds In Head, Neck And Chest.
   Two Wounds Made One Hour After Death.

3. Gun was 'Lina's own' say Police.
   'Daughter, 10, Saw It All But Has Been Struck Dumb By Trauma.'

4. 'Lovely Lina' had been separated from Hank 'Happy' Hapgood for two years and they were involved in a bitter custody battle over daughter, Lucy. Hapgood is known to have 'gangland connections' and Lina was considering divorce on grounds of mental cruelty, says Hollywood Gossip, Latish Ludlow.
   'She told me she was going to pay him off so he'd leave Lina and Lucy alone. Lina was a devoted mother.'

5. LINA SHOOTING: WAS THERE 'ANOTHER MAN'?
   Happy Hapgood had told friends the faded star was setting up with another man. Jockey Titch Tupelo has been named in several gossip columns as a possible ...

6. TITCH TUPELO DENIES LOVE LIES
   Jockey, Titch Tupelo stood at his wife's side today and denied any involvement with ex-glamour queen, Lina Lamont.
   'I met her just the one time. She was a nice lady but kind of wild.'

7. FANS RIOT AS HAPPY WEEPS AT LINA'S FUNERAL

8. HAPPY HAPGOOD IN SUICIDE ATTEMPT

9. Happy Hapgood, husband of murdered movie star, Lina Lamont, was today was released into her sister-in-law's custody.
   Mrs Penny Shilling said she was convinced of Hapgood's innocence and both she and her husband, longshoreman, Mitch, would also look after daughter, Lucy.
   'We are simple, decent folk but we will give Lucy a good home.'

10. HAPPY HAPGOOD FOUND DEAD
    BODY 'RIDDLED WITH BULLETS'
    MUTE DAUGHTER MISSING

11. MISSING LUCY FOUND IN RAILWAY CARRIAGE MILES FROM HOME

12. AUNT ARRESTED FOR MURDER OF HAPPY HAPGOOD.
    HE DESERVED TO DIE, SHE SCREAMED AT POLICE

13. LUCY WEEPS AT HAPPY'S GRAVE

14. LUCY BREAKS DOWN IN COURT AS AUNT CONFESSES

15. PENNY SHILLING HEARS DEATH PENALTY AS LINA'S LAST MOVIE BREAKS BOX OFFICE RECORDS

I have summarised this lurid patchwork of a story in 15 points. There is, on the surface, a degree of clarity and logic to these events, but if I allow myself to think more deeply about them – and I would have to do so to turn them into a novel – I would have to expand the plan to 20 or even 30 points.

There are questions which go unanswered in the above sequence and, by attempting to list and answer them, I will be able to expand my plan and explore the material further.

First, I might consider what has led to the killing of Lina Lamont. How did she and Happy meet? What is the story of their marriage? What led to the breakdown in the marriage? A battle over custody, we are told, and, possibly, even another man – but are we being told the truth? What did Titch Tupelo mean when he described Lina as 'kind of wild' and what can be made of Happy's gangland connections?

I might ask myself if I need to record in some detail what leads up to this killing – the early lives of these characters – or would it be better to begin with the short dramatic scene of the shooting and then slip back in time to suggest how it might have come about?

I might even ponder the time and place in which these events took place. This story is set in 1930s Hollywood and it would mean researching the period and the industry. The story could, however, be transplanted. It could be set in the world of the theatre or the contemporary music scene or even a small town in the United States, perhaps at the turn of the century. Could I transplant these events nearer my own time or even further back? What would be gained by this and what would be lost?

When I come to the first killing, I have to ask 'Why is there a gun in the house?' Did Happy really kill Lina? Might it have been a suicide? What about the 10-year-old daughter? What was her involvement in the tragedy? How does she feel about her father, her mother, her aunt? Is she traumatized or is she keeping silent for some other reason? Could she have killed Lina? Why would a daughter want to kill her mother?

There is 'the other man' to consider but does he exist? The only evidence for his existence in the newspaper cuttings are the claims made by Happy to his friends. If he does exist, who is he? Is it Titch Tupelo? What is his story? Is there another plot here, a subplot?

There is also the aunt, Penny Shilling, a late entrant in the plot, but what is her story and how does it entwine with that of her successful sister? Can she be introduced earlier? What is her opinion of Happy and why, seemingly, does it change so radically and suddenly? Again there is another story lurking here, another subplot perhaps. How will all these stories tie up?

In planning, I would be looking for symmetry and balance, echoes, anomalies, holes that are begging to be filled. Whatever I might add, I think I might try to keep the scene of Happy at Lina's grave and then his attempted suicide the centrally placed event in the novel. It sums up the consequences of one killing (Lina's) and sets the action up for another (Happy's) and a novel that has one character's murder at its beginning, another at its climax and another (Penny's execution) as its conclusion, has, at its pivot, a character's attempt to kill herself.

The questions you can pose are endless and the answers multiply but throughout I am looking for symmetry in the way the story is told, unpleating the material to see how much there is. While I think and plan, I am free to invent, to follow any line and then erase it. Take pleasure in this freedom.

Expanding

- Take the above plot and expand it into 20 or 25 points.
- Think of a subplot featuring Titch – or whoever you think 'the other man' might be – and another subplot that features Penny Shilling. At present both of these characters figure either at the beginning or at the end of the action. Conjure up ways in which their stories can weave in and out of the main plot so that it either complements or contrasts with them.
- Need you plan chronologically? What if you started at the end – Penny's trial – and moved backwards? Or perhaps begin with a central event – Happy at his wife's grave – and weave back and forth.
- Having done these things with an established story, do these things with your own idea for a novel. See what fits and what does not.
- You might try storyboarding your novel by taking a stack of cards and jotting down an image or scene on each one. When you have a sufficient number of these cards, say 20, lay them out in a sequence and 'then turn your thoughts to any gaps and let new ideas occur to you'.[4] This approach may help you conceive a new chronology for the events in the story.

You are free to do whatever you want when you are planning a story. You are trying to discover what works. You need not sit at a desk to do any of these exercises but dream them, eyes open. Everything is provisional.

But, remember, if story is important to you, always ask if what you are writing is moving the plot on. A story need not stand still while you concentrate on describing a character or an idea. Such things are your story.

CHARACTERIZATION

You may have a tendency to write from your own experience, but it is not always wise to do so directly. If you are writing or dealing with material that is directly autobiographical, try to create a distance between you and the character who is closest to you. Let it become other.

You can start by writing a summary of your life so far and then shift the point of view to your sibling, your partner, your friend. How would they have lived your life? What you do by such an exercise is make your life 'other'. You are thinking about your past not as you lived it but as a character might have lived it.

Why not fill out a questionnaire for your characters which includes the following:

- name (and maiden name, if applicable)
- address
- date of birth
- a detailed physical description
- parents, names and histories
- relationship to family members
- education
- job
- salary
- interests
- fears
- prejudices
- desires
- attitudes
- friends
- enemies.

You might never use most of this information but it will give you confidence and make you feel you know your characters.

Dorothea Brande recommends that you go for a walk and interview your character, grill them about what they think of the other characters, about what is happening to them, and even about events outside your novel.[5] Get them to speak to you and listen to the way they use language and observe how they might use such and such a gesture to accompany a particular phrase.

Most importantly, you must spend time thinking about your characters and relating what you decide about them to what the plot demands of them. Action comes out of character and character is revealed in action. You must make them fit.

In a novel you are not recording life but re-creating it, not presenting it but re-presenting it. In life, people do not have to display a consistent character. In life, the pale man who cultivates orchids can chop up his wife and children and never have to account for himself. If this man were one of your characters, his actions would have to be consistent within the world of the novel. You have to account for him.

A wife should not leave a husband primarily because your plot demands it. Each character should have an inner motive. In the Lina Lamont plot there are at least two murders. If Happy kills Lina because she was unfaithful, you must make us believe why he would do this. Not every partner kills a cheating spouse. What makes Happy react in this way? What is it in his nature, his relationships, not only with Lina but also with those around him, that makes murder seem inevitable?

Avoid judging a character too directly. It gives the reader nothing to do. Often the most effective way to move a reader to tears or horror is to describe the character while denying yourself the very emotion you wish to inspire. Practise by writing down an action you find physically or morally repugnant and try to describe it without judgement, or betraying how you feel about it.

Show, don't tell

Introduce your characters with a flourish. Establish them physically and immediately if you can. Instead of telling us about them, show them and dramatize them.

Go through your address book and write down three physical gestures, features or turns of phrase that typify each person. Avoid bland or generalized terms such as fat, pretty, nice. Go for 'lop-sided smile … eyebrows almost permanently raised as if surprised to be in the world at all'.

POINT OF VIEW

Point of view (or POV) is about who is telling your story. It is one of the most crucial decisions you will make in response to the material you wish to turn into a novel. For a detailed discussion of your choices consult the relevant section in Chapter 6, 'Short story writing'.

DIALOGUE

In everyday life we speak too imprecisely and at too great a length to serve a novelist's purpose. In novels, dialogue is a re-presentation of what we say in life, an edited highlight that must sound faithful, real.

* Write down a conversation between two people who are making up after a serious argument. Make it last for at least 750 words.
* A page of film script takes, on average, a minute to film. Imagine that you need this conversation but cannot afford to spend two minutes of screentime on it. You must reduce it to 30 seconds – by at least a quarter, and more if possible – yet the scene must still work.

Unlike a scriptwriter, a novelist can resort to reported speech, but it can be very distancing, so the summarized conversation is best reduced to its essentials.

Avoid being too faithful to speech or using phonetic spellings. Novelists often veer into caricature when they do so. Indicate accent or dialect by rhythm and vocabulary – dropped h's are painful to read and often indicate a patronizing attitude, although strong dialect, as in the best Scots writers, needs no justification.

Get into the habit of reading your dialogue aloud, or go for a walk playing your latest chapter on a personal stereo. It is a good way of making it other, of becoming your own reader, of taking words off the page and into that private place inside a reader's head where all the best novels come alive.

Avoid too much 'he said, she said' and do not depend on its variations such as 'he questioned', 'she responded', 'he averred', etc. Use the 'he said, she said' construction to avoid confusion and vary it only if you want to convey a shift in mood such as 'she laughed' or 'he snapped at her'. If you need to add 'she screamed', ask yourself why your dialogue does not convey this in its own right. Look at how little direction a playwright gives as to how a line should be said. Remember, too, that dialogue accompanied by a description of gesture or physical detail can be very effective. Often we do not say what we mean and it is our bodies that betray our true intention. Study this exchange:

A   You're late.
B   Sorry.
A   My car ran out of petrol.
B   Did it?
A   Has the film started?
B   Yes. Did you really want to see it?
A   Yes, of course.

Now rewrite it indicating that:

- A is angry and B is lying
- A is secretly amused and B is genuinely apologetic
- neither A nor B care either about being late or missing the film – they are just glad to be together.

WRITING WITH AN INTENTION

Most first drafts are either underwritten or overwritten and usually both in varying proportions. It would be a surprise if they were not. Do not worry about this so much that it stops your flow but, if the draft feels sketchy, ask yourself if you have sufficiently kept your reader in mind. If you know a landscape really well, you may not have bothered to describe it to a newcomer. You may not have communicated it.

Identify your intention in your novel as a whole and each scene in particular. You will probably have more than one aim, so decide which is the main one. Carol Clewlow says you should ask yourself what is the one thing that you want to do in this scene and then concentrate on just doing that – the rest, she says, will follow if you let it.

If you were to write the novel suggested by the Lina Lamont killings your main theme might be, say, to show how people are imprisoned by relationships. You may have other things to say and to do – establish character, move the story on, describe the wallpaper – but, if you kept your main intention firmly and uppermost in mind, you know that in that first scene – the shooting of Lina Lamont – you most want to give an example of a family who once loved each other but are now trapped into hating each other. What you then choose to say about them, and what you choose to have them say to each other, would be coloured by this intention, this theme of imprisonment. You could look at the house in which the killing took place, how the moonlight comes through the blinds and stripes the walls like prison bars, what it must be like to be a small girl – perhaps hiding inside a cupboard – watching her parents argue, unable to do anything about it, and how Happy feels compelled to do what he does and how Lina acts as if she had no choice but to say and do things which provoke him into such terrible violence.

Though the advice may seem paradoxical in the light of the above paragraph, an intention is best illustrated with restraint. Do not so much disguise it as imply it. The French novelist Stendhal suggested that you find out what you most want to say and then try very hard not to say it. Writing with a secret agenda gives prose a pulse, a hidden but real sense of animation.

The mystery barn

The novelist and tutor John Gardner suggests as an exercise trying to describe a barn as seen by a man whose son has just been killed in a war. Do not, he says, mention the son or the war or death. 'If worked on hard enough, a wonderful image will be evoked, a real barn would stand before us but one filled with mysterious meaning.'[6]

Gardner also suggests trying to describe a lake as seen by a young man who has murdered his girlfriend. Do not mention the murder.

STYLE

The hunt for a style that expresses you, fulfils the many functions a novel has to perform, and that pleases the reader is a lifelong pursuit, and one of the aims you can pursue in redrafting (see Chapter 16). Your first drafts are allowed to be messy, sketchy and inadequate, but every now and then try writing each sentence separately, leaving a line on each side of it. This allows you to look at each sentence, see how long it is, how rhythmic, or, even, necessary – and the space around it gives you the space later to fiddle and rewrite it.

Style, characterization, structure, point of view, dialogue all need to be worked on. Novels demand time and work and will reward both. Writing a novel entails a great deal of working back and forth between the small detail of the novel that makes it real and the general shape that holds all these details in place. You must think of everything all the time, attend to plot and to character, make sure dialogue is convincing and that the prose is expressing what you wish it to do. You will, as David Mamet puts it, 'let one thing predominate for a while and then come back to it so that eventually what you do, like a pastry chef, is frost your mistakes if you can'.[7]

Your novel will be finished when you and it agree it is. Once you have drafted it comes the work of redrafting. Be patient. Work hard. Work well. Happy frosting.

Notes

1 'Don de Lillo, the Art of Fiction CXXXV', *Paris Review*, issue 128 (autumn 1993).
2 *Writers at Work: The Paris Review Interviews*, fourth series (Penguin, Harmondsworth, 1977).
3 D. H. Lawrence, *Collected Letters*, vol. 1 (Heinemann, London, 1962).
4 Crawford Kilian's website has many useful tips on novel writing and is worth investigating: Crawford Kilian, 'Storyboarding' Crawford-Kilian@mindlink.bc.ca
5 Dorothea Brande, *Becoming a Writer* (Macmillan, London, 1983).
6 John Gardner, *The Art of Fiction* (Alfred A. Knopf, New York, 1984).
7 'David Mamet, the Art of the Theater XI', *Paris Review*, issue 135 (spring 1997).

Part Three:
Branching out

12 SONG LYRIC WRITING

Dave Jackson

There are no rules to song writing. As soon as you try to say songs are this or songs are that, someone writes a song that breaks the mould.

COMMUNICATION

Like any other area of creative writing, song lyric writing is first and foremost about communication. What the lyricist wants to communicate will differ from writer to writer and song to song. Some politically motivated singer/songwriters feel obliged to use their creativity to try and change the world. To them, the generic love song disguises its true nature. Others would not dream of writing a song that did not tell a tale of new love found or old love lost. And others like to tell us horror stories or write slice-of-life mini-dramas. Then there are those songs which, if you take the lyrics at face value, mean nothing; but in the context of the music and the way they are sung seem to tap into something mythic.

The audience for songs is just as diverse. Some people are very word-orientated and will follow song writing which places heavy emphasis on language, but most people are not, and seem to just hear an overall soundscape.

Favourite lyrics

Think about your favourite song lyrics. Why do they appeal to you? Is it their clever word-play? Is it the simplicity of the sentiments or ideas expressed? Do the words intrigue or mystify you? Do they blend with the music or work against it, drawing attention to themselves as lyrics? Do the lyrics tell a story? Do they open up a new world or a different perspective on the world? Do they seem to speak to you directly? Do they affect you emotionally? If so, how?

Think about the type of songs you like and the type of lyrics you would like to write. Make some notes. Different writers have different ideas on what works best. Some lyricists trust their first inspiration and believe in getting a song written as quickly as possible. Others, like Leonard Cohen, will labour over certain songs for months or even years, rejecting countless verses until they have got the right ones.

WHAT TO WRITE

Some songwriters seem to write solely from personal experience, about things that have happened to them, often unrequited love. Others find writing about themselves is too personal or too subjective.

It is probably best to be as flexible as possible. Try writing short rhyming stories about incidents or people you know or have read about. Write from different characters' perspectives. Randy Newman, for instance, always writes in the first person but in the voice of an adopted persona, usually an 'untrustworthy narrator'. You can always sneak bits of confessional material into your songs and pretend they are about someone else. I know a writer who used to sit in front of the television making notes of images and things that were said, looking for random connections, chance meetings that would act as a source of inspiration. Films, novels, poetry, comics, paintings, photographs, computer games – anything can spark an idea.

Some writers approach lyric writing as an act of discovery. Rather than know what the song is going to say in advance and plotting it methodically, they develop the song from a few key words or phrases, using the metre of the melody line to give it forward motion.

Sometimes simple serendipity can be the spark point for an idea. One contemporary songwriter tells a story of how he was in a pub when a guitarist from his band arrived. The guitarist told him he had just been to see the French film, *Manon des Sources*. His French pronunciation, however, left much to be desired. The songwriter could not help asking, 'Man on the sauce? Is it about a heavy drinker?' He decided to write a song called 'Man on the Sauce'. As soon as the guitarist presented him with a riff on which to base the vocal, the lyrics seemed to write themselves.

Picking a subject

From the notes you made earlier, pick a subject for a song. Write a page of prose on the subject. Sort out the bits you want to make into a song. Pick an existing song that you know well, and using its melody, metre and rhyming structure, write a new set of lyrics for it from your subject matter.

As you continue to write songs you should always be reacting and
making corrections to your last piece of writing. In this way, you will
start to develop an awareness and a style. Some songs can be abstract
and others very precise, some dreamlike, others gritty and down to earth.
You can even contrast the one with the other within the same song. You
could, for instance, have a gritty verse balanced by a surreal chorus.

LISTEN

You should listen to lots of different types of song. Listen to as much
current music as you can, but also listen to old standards, like the cleverly
crafted songs of Cole Porter, Oscar Hammerstein and Sammy Cahn.
Listen to the blues of Robert Johnson and Willie Dixon, the country music
of Hank Williams and the Louvin Brothers, or the folk music of Woody
Guthrie and Pete Seeger. Listen to Hal David's lyrical collaborations with
Burt Bacharach like 'Alfie' and 'Walk on By'. Listen to Leonard Cohen,
Bob Dylan and the Beatles. Listen to the different ways these writers
make their lyrics work.

SING

Always sing your lyrics aloud. It does not matter if you think you have
got the worst voice in the world, you need to sing the words to see if they
work. Some words or lines that seem to work on paper may be difficult to
sing. Do you allow the singer room to breathe?

Metre in songs is easier to find when you sing them aloud. Many lyricists do not have to think about what they are doing. The process just seems
instinctive, like talking. What we tend to forget is that we had to learn to
talk. Learn to sing. Re-read the section on metre in Chapter 8. Sing other
people's songs and find the stressed syllables that make up the metre. Sing
your own compositions. Be honest with yourself. How do they compare?

Sing while you are walking. Walking has been a source of inspiration
to lyricists as diverse as Pete Townshend and Oscar Hammerstein. The
rhythm and forward motion seem somehow suited to the activity of
songwriting. Sing in the car. It is useful to learn your own songs by rote,
especially if you are going to perform them yourself.

TUNES

If you write your own music, this obviously makes writing lyrics easier.
Having the tune to hand or even just in your head is important. The

melody and rhythm dictate the metre of the lyrics. You do not have to be a musician to write song lyrics. But non-musicians need to collaborate with musicians.

Some lyricists try to cram their words into the structure of unsuitable tunes. If you are not writing the music yourself, work closely with your collaborator(s). The musician might write a melody line for your lyric to follow. Alternatively, you may improvise vocal lines to a guitar riff or a keyboard line. It helps to have a melodic or rhythmic structure to build your lyrics around.

You may prefer to tape the music and take it away, to try out different sets of lyrics and vocal lines in private. You may also want to try making up your own vocal melodies. You can then sing the finished lyrics to a patient musician or musicians, who will dutifully work out the chords.

TITLES AND THEMES

Many songwriters recommend finding a title first and using it to work out the theme (the 'Man on the Sauce' example being a case in point). Others start with a theme and let the title emerge with the song.

A generally accepted principle, however, is that individual songs should be about one subject, theme or concept. The most popular songs seem to be about fairly universal themes such as love. The trick is to approach the subject from a fresh angle.

A song I admire by Smog is called 'Ex-Con'. It is not actually about an ex-con, but someone who feels like one when he puts on a tie to meet his girlfriend's family. The title acts as a plant which pays off within the body of the song. It has been said that you can sum up the theme or story of a good song in a few words.

REPETITION OF KEY WORDS, VERSES AND CHORUSES

Many songs have what is known as a hook. This is usually a short phrase which has a rhythmic beat or idea which is repeated. Look for elements in the words that can be repeated – a chorus, an important verse or a line. A lot of songs repeat the title several times. Give people something to remember even after one hearing. You are trying to hypnotize your audience and draw them into your own little three-to-five-minute world. Repetition is an effective way to do this. As a rule, it is advisable not to make a song too long. Sometimes, even I drift off after a couple of minutes into 'Sad-eyed Lady of the Lowlands'. Try and grab the listener's attention immediately, in the first few words. You only have a very limited time.

DETAIL

Being specific about detail lends your writing a sense of authenticity. Rather than just singing about a man or a woman, give them a name. Say what type of expensive car you want the Lord to buy you. Tell us that you met her at 'St Martin's College' or focus on her 'Leopard-skin Pillbox Hat'.

CLICHÉS

Clichés and obvious rhymes abound in popular song. Sometimes the use of a cliché in an otherwise original lyric can be quite effective. Greg Milton came up with an effective inversion of a cliché in his song 'House by the Airport'. The song detailing the collapse of a marriage first talks about the husband having a 'sense of doing something right for the girl' but later dryly mentions that 'He had a foot in every pie and a finger in every door'.

Many song titles are clichés ('Accidents Will Happen') sometimes twisted for effect. Some become clichés ('The times they are a changin'). However, if you fill your songs with too many of them, you run the risk of sounding banal and absurd.

OBVIOUS RHYMES

Often, when you listen to songs for the first time, you are able to anticipate the next line. Sometimes the obviousness can be used to good effect, in order to go against the grain of a lyric. But, more often, lyricists put in a line that rhymes simply to finish the song. This gives it an aura of triteness and inaccuracy and may ruin what may otherwise be a powerful lyric. Obvious rhymes are clichés too. Try not to overdo them. Jonathan Richman uses a technique whereby he sets the listener up to expect an obvious rhyme and does not rhyme the next line at all. This, sparingly used, can be quite effective.

The real danger for songwriters is in combining all the elements of unoriginality. Writers of folk songs, for instance, may claim that although their songs may not have very original tunes, they are saved by effective lyrics. Some songs have trite lyrics with many obvious rhymes, but have such an interesting tune, melody or rhythm that this does not appear to matter, and the song becomes popular.

It can be difficult to consider lyrics in isolation from the tune. Many songs, loved by millions, have really uninteresting, pedestrian lyrics.

Even with all the clichés combined, the performance or production of a song can make all the difference. Some extremely original songwriters do not know how to present their work and fail to inspire much interest. Others perform their trite material so well they can hold an audience spellbound. How else do you account for the Spice Girls?

13 TRAVEL WRITING

Aileen La Tourette

Since God first created man no Christian, Pagan, Tartar, Indian or person of any other race has explored every part of the world as thoroughly as Marco Polo, nor seen so many of its wonders. He himself thought it would be wrong not to keep a record of the marvellous things he had seen and heard so that people who knew nothing about them could learn from this book.[1]

INTRODUCTION

Travel writing has taken off in our time – pun intended. More people travel now than at any other time in history. The reasons why people travel appear at first glance to have changed quite a bit. We might say that we travel for leisure and relaxation, rather than out of necessity or to go on a pilgrimage to a sacred site.

But if we look more closely, our reasons for travel resemble our ancestors'. We, too, travel in order to satisfy a restless craving we may not be able to define. The same craving, the same restlessness, sent explorers out across uncharted seas. Pilgrims often visited shrines in order to do penance for their sins, but they often enjoyed their penitential journeys so much that the church began to frown on them.

We have our own forms of pilgrimage. People travel to Graceland in Tennessee, to Brontë country in Yorkshire, to Père Lachaise cemetery in Paris, to pay homage to mythic figures from the past. They leave tokens of their affection and esteem. Travelling to a site which is special to us in some way seems to satisfy a basic human need, and telling each other about our adventures along the way seems to satisfy another. Think of Chaucer's *Canterbury Tales*, made up of characters on pilgrimage and the stories they tell each other to while away the time. Another kind of pilgrimage is a memory journey. Someone may travel to the country of their ancestors, or to a place they once lived themselves, and remember clearly, or vaguely, or not at all. Or they may make a pilgrimage to a war cemetery to find the grave of a father, grandfather or great-grandfather.

Personal pilgrimage

Write an account of a pilgrimage you have made in your own life. You probably did not call it that at the time, or think of it in that way, but that does not matter. It may have been a pilgrimage to a football stadium or a restaurant. Write about the anticipation with which you began your journey. What was it that drew you to this particular place? See if you can untangle the roots of its fascination for you. What happened when you got there? Was it what you expected? Better? Worse? Be truthful, and include all the details you can remember, as clearly and specifically as you remember them.

HITTING THE ROAD

'... the road is life'.[2]

Everyone by now has heard the old Chinese saying, 'A journey of a thousand miles starts with a single step.' In travel writing, we start with the journey. In his book – and tapes – *The Old Patagonian Express*,[3] Paul Theroux talks about setting off for his journey on a commuter train. He reflects on the difference between himself and the other travellers, namely that for him the ordinary commuter train is the first step of a great adventure, while to them it is simply a shuttle to work. He is isolating a major factor in tourist travel, and one that helps to make it the enormous source of energy and re-creation that it is: the fact that travel offers a break from routine, a change. Human beings are creatures of habit, and we very quickly become acclimatized or adjusted to our surroundings. This is a useful trait – it has helped us to survive – but it can also result in a loss of awareness, a kind of numbness. If we just go through the motions and do not look around us, life is very dull. Travel, and travel writing, should help to get us out of our rut.

The methods of travel are fascinating. Some people hitch, some travel by bicycle, or motorbike, some walk amazing distances. People travel by kayak, by ocean liner, by trains of various kinds. All these methods have their delights and their delays as well as their frustrations and difficulties.

Bon voyage?

Write about a journey – only the journey, not the arrival – that you have taken. Think about car journeys you might have taken with your parents and siblings as a kid. Write about the fights that broke out in the back seat or the front, the carsickness, the flat tyres. Think about the monotony and the hypnotism of long train journeys, the conversations with strangers, or the silences, and the conjectures you make about your fellow travellers. Do not forget to include titbits you may have overheard while travelling, or sights you might have seen in a bus station or from a window. Listen to the music of travel, songs about crossing America by Simon and Garfunkel, for example. Write about as many different kinds of travel as you can. Remember to include examples like the donkey rides you might have had as a child, even the piggy-back rides you remember. We are talking about locomotion here, and what it felt like. When you run out of forms of transport known to you, try to imagine one that is unknown. What would it feel like to waft about in a hot-air balloon, or climb the air in a helicopter? Try to find an account of the exotic form of travel you have chosen, and see how it compares with your imaginary one.

WHEREVER YOU GO, THERE YOU ARE

The best travel writers take us on an inward journey as well as an outward one. This does not mean that a travel writer is always in the way, like someone who brings back a photo album of snapshots with their own figure always in the foreground, blocking the landscape from view. It simply means that they are filtering everything through their own personality and their own sensibilities, and the writing carries a strong flavour of their particular attitudes, their unique point of view. Often, travel writers will use a journal to take us along with them and to keep a record of their travels. Refer back to the chapter on journals to remind yourself of how they work. Journals are personal by definition. No one can cram in every single detail they meet in the course of a day, or a journey. The process of selection is highly subjective and revealing.

Travel writing is different from guidebooks. It makes no attempt to be objective. It is not reportage. That does not mean that a travel writer is free to air prejudices – far from it. But it does mean that instead of pretending to be like a camera's eye, totally neutral – and even a camera's eye has the photographer's eye behind it – the travel writer makes a feature of subjectivity. No two people ever see the same thing, however hard they look. So paint your own pictures in your travel writing. Deliver your own impressions, without worrying about what you 'should' think.

No place like home

Go on a journey down your own street. Think about what you know and do not know about it, and about the other people who live there. Try to notice at least five things you have never noticed before. Travel and travel writing both try to make us look at things again, as all good writing should do. In order for this to work, you, the travel writer, must learn to look at things around you in a fresh way.

Now write a travel piece about your street. Show it to someone else who lives there, if you can, perhaps someone in your family, and see if they agree with you or not. They may point out things you have left out, or question things you have included. All writing is selective. You will put in what you think is important, what you feel makes the place you live what it is. If your reader reacts to something you have mentioned in the piece by saying 'You know, I never noticed that', you will know you have succeeded.

Where am I?

Keep a travel journal for a week. Detail every journey you make. Include maps and illustrations, snapshots or pictures. Talk about the 'souvenirs' you bring back, like fluff from a carpet. Make the smallest, most banal or disgusting detail amusing and alive.

GETTING LOST

'We know all too well that few journeys are linear and predictable. Instead they swerve and turn, twist and double back, until we don't know if we are coming or going.'[4]

The experience of getting lost is universal. Children get lost in supermarkets, in shopping centres, in forests. Getting lost has a kind of mythic resonance, like travel itself. In myths, the hero must often set out on a journey, a quest. In the course of the quest, the hero is often lost. There must be a sign, a clue, a miracle, to bring the quest to a joyful conclusion.

So the traveller, whatever the quest of a particular journey, often gets lost. It may be that getting lost was part of the purpose of the journey, that life had become a little bit too stale or 'found'. Tales of getting lost and then found read like little fairy tales, miniature myths inside travel writing.

Hide and seek

Bring to mind an experience you have had of getting lost. Try to re-live the panic you felt when you realized you were lost. What did you do? Where were you? Remember how threatening your surroundings looked, wherever you were. Being lost makes everything look darker and bigger than it is. Were you cold, or hot? Hungry? Tired? How did you react? Write your getting-lost story, concentrating on two things: (1) your sense impressions – everything you saw, heard, touched, tasted and felt while you were lost; and (2) the atmosphere of the place you were in, both while you were lost in it and when you were found again. See how the place changes for you when it is no longer threat-ening. Also be aware of how strange you feel to yourself when you are lost – as if you were no longer you.

GOING FURTHER

'The only aspect of our travels that is guaranteed to hold an audi-ence is disaster.'[5]

The stories in the ground-breaking anthology *Fortune Hotel*[6] are primarily about trips which for one reason or another are disastrous. The book describes itself as 'alternative travel writing' and is an antidote to traditional narratives in which travel is always exciting and exhilarating and 'adventure' is a much overworked word. Likewise, Anne Tyler's novel *The Accidental Tourist*,[7] which was made into a film starring William Hurt, uses a certain kind of travel as a symbol of an emotional condition. The central character writes guidebooks for business travellers. He tries to spare them as much hassle as possible, and ends by sparing them the experience of travel as well, just as he has arranged his own life in such a way as to spare himself the inconvenience of feeling.

The American travel writer Peter Matthiessen travels into the Himalayas in search of a wonderful animal in his book *The Snow Leopard*.[8] It is a kind of quest. He is filled with the desire to see this rare animal. In the course of the book, he meditates on many things in his life while tracking the elusive leopard. He sometimes gets very close to it, but he never actually sees it, and he begins to realize the significance of the journey itself, and the reflections it brought about, not in a sentimental 'silver lining' kind of way, but in a profound way. If you go back to the accounts of Marco Polo's travels, which you should, you will find rich descriptions of every kind of obstacle, not all of which are overcome. The wonderful stories of Victorian women travellers are filled with details which emphasize the hazards of travel as well as the delights. Caryl Churchill in her play *Top Girls*[9] uses Isabella Bird, one of the best-known

Victorian woman travellers, as a character in the first act of the play, which assembles famous women from the past. Isabella Bird's speeches make us aware of the many ills from which she suffered, or thought she suffered, which makes it all the more amazing that she travelled as much and as intrepidly as she did. Her speeches also remind us of another motive for travel, besides restlessness and the desire to visit a shrine – sheer escapism.

P. J. O'Rourke's book *Holidays in Hell*[10] tells of visits to unlikely and unappealing places like Chernobyl, and Martha Gellhorn's *Travels with Myself and Another*[11] is an earlier example of a travel book which is completely hilarious in its recital of woes. Bill Bryson's travel books are filled with wry accounts of disasters and near-disasters on the road, and Joseph O'Connor's *Sweet Liberty: Travels in Irish America*[12] sets out to explore places in the US with Irish names, only to discover that most of the inhabitants of such places are completely ignorant of their Irish heritage and totally indifferent to it.

Disasters

Think of a disastrous journey of your own. It might be a romantic or a family holiday that went wrong. Write a list of all the details that made it catastrophic. Now write a piece about it, exaggerating rather than playing down the things you have listed. See how much more interesting it is than a cosy travel story where everything goes according to plan.

The important thing is not to be too high-minded about your disasters. If you got into a fight in a bar and ended up having to run for your life, say so. If you were drunk as a skunk at the time, tell us that, too.

FOLLOWING IN THE FOOTPRINTS OF ...

Another kind of travel writing involves following in the footprints of another traveller, repeating their journey. This way you are doing homage to the original traveller(s) and also giving yourself a particular kind of journey. You may feel you are in touch with the person whose itinerary you are following in an intimate kind of way. The poets Simon Armitage and Glyn Maxwell did this, repeating the journey that W. H. Auden and Christopher Isherwood made to Antarctica. They tell the story of their journey and recap details of the original one in their book *Moon Country*.[13] Alan Hankinson traces Coleridge's footsteps in his book *Coleridge Walks the Fells: A Lakeland Journey Retraced*.[14] Sometimes these repeat journeys have a melancholic side to them, as the contemporary traveller faces a far more overcrowded landscape than the original traveller ever dreamed of or, even more seriously, detects signs and symptoms of ecological deterioration. Many travel books include details of the destruction of our planet and its inhabitants.

Follow the leader

Find an account of a journey you particularly like the sound of, one that is not beyond your geographical reach, but which belongs to another time. It can be an account from travel writing as such or from fiction – an account of a part of London from Dickens, for example. Go in the footsteps of the character or travel writer, and see if you can see what they saw. You may have to use your imagination, if the place is entirely transformed. Now write an account of your journey, detailing all the changes that have taken place since the original journey was made.

WHEN IN ROME ...

Yet another kind of traveller goes into another community and lives its life for a time, or tries to. This is a demanding and engrossing form of travel. It involves not only physical travel but an attempt to actually be part of another culture. Examples of this kind of travel are *Mutant Message Down Under: A Woman's Journey into Dreamtime Australia* by Marlo Morgan,[15] and *Thank You and OK! An American Zen Failure in Japan*, by David Chadwick.[16] In each of these books, the author has attempted to live as one of the people he or she is visiting. Marlo Morgan describes a privileged period spent on walkabout with aborigines in Australia, and the enormous respect she felt for their way of life. David Chadwick talks about Zen and his own struggle with it, and with Japan.

Fitting in

Think of a time in your life when you had to assimilate with what was, to you, a foreign culture. It can be as simple and domestic as your attempts to 'fit in' when you first went to school. Remember the strange signs you had to learn to interpret, the new language you had to learn. Perhaps you grew up in two different households. What adjustments did you have to make in each one?

If you have ever travelled as a student, or even gone to a foreign restaurant where you were confused by the menu, flavours and customs that surrounded you, you can write about these experiences. The main thing is that you do not assume that anyone is 'right' or 'wrong'. Simply tell us what it felt like to be the stranger, the one out of step, and how you coped.

RELUCTANT VOYAGERS

Many people travel because they have no choice. Sometimes we are forced to take journeys out of hardship and sorrow. We are removed from the things that normally give us a sense of who we are – and from familiar people.

No choice

Think of a reluctant journey in your own life, like a journey to hospital or boarding school. It must be a journey which involved you in a loss of control over the routine of your own days and nights. You may have had to wear special clothing, or depend on a small supply of clothing which you brought with you. You may have been out of touch with people you were used to seeing all the time, unable to contact them, or only able to do so at certain times. Write an account of this sojourn, wherever it was, without self-pity but clearly and precisely.

SELLING THE PIECE

Many people want to be travel writers. The chief reward of the job is the opportunity it affords to travel and be paid for it – so the competition is stiff. You will have to offer something original. I do not mean that you have to hang-glide your way around the world or bungee-jump in every major city. But your point of view, your intent in setting out, will have to have a slant that interests an editor.

Do not be afraid to start with your local paper. There might be walks you can take around your own area that an editor will publish, if you write them up interestingly enough. Include conversations with eccentric locals, especially elderly ones, with sprinklings of oral history and accounts of how things used to be.

You are unlikely to be handed huge budgets for travel expenses right away. Make use of all your travel opportunities. Try to find something other people have overlooked. Try to approach your destinations with humour, with openness, with a willingness to be astonished or disappointed or enthralled – or bored silly, as Martha Gellhorn was with Bali. Like all writing, travel writing demands that you be yourself, but not any old self – your worst self or your best, your most outrageous or your most depraved. Human beings are endlessly curious about each other and about the world. Make the most of that precious curiosity.

Notes

1 Marco Polo, *The Travels of Marco Polo, A Modern Translation by Teresa Waugh from the Italian by Maria Bellonci* (Sidgwick and Jackson, London, 1984).
2 Jack Kerouac, *On the Road*, quoted in *A Book of Travellers' Tales* assembled by Eric Newby (Picador, London, 1986).
3 Paul Theroux, *The Old Patagonian Express* (Penguin, Harmondsworth, 1996).
4 Phil Cousineau, *The Art of Pilgrimage* (Element Books, Shaftesbury, Dorset, 1999).
5 Martha Gellhorn, *Travels with Myself and Another* (Eland, London, 1983).
6 Sarah Champion, *Fortune Hotel* (Penguin, Harmondsworth, 1995).
7 Anne Tyler, *The Accidental Tourist* (Vintage, New York, 1995).
8 Peter Matthiessen, *The Snow Leopard* (Pan, London, 1975).
9 Caryl Churchill, *Top Girls* (Methuen, London, 1991).
10 P. J. O'Rourke, *Holidays in Hell* (Picador, London, 1989).
11 Gellhorn, *Travels with Myself and Another*.
12 Joseph O'Connor, *Sweet Liberty: Travels in Irish America* (Picador, London, 1997).
13 Simon Armitage and Glyn Maxwell, *Moon Country* (Faber and Faber, London, 1996).
14 Alan Hankinson, *Coleridge Walks the Fells: A Lakeland Journey Retraced* (Ellenbank, Maryport, Cumbria, 1991).
15 Marlo Morgan, *Mutant Message Down Under: A Woman's Journey into Dreamtime Australia* (Thorsons, London, 1995).
16 David Chadwick, *Thank You and OK! An American Zen Failure in Japan* (Penguin, Arkana, 1994).

14 WRITING ON THE WEB
James Friel

INTRODUCTION

The world wide web is a writer's resource. It offers you, among many other things, access to libraries, workshops, noticeboards, writing tuition, travel guides, archives, a post office, marketing information, a new way of writing and a showcase for your work. It can ease the loneliness of a writer's life by connecting you to other writers, and it can get you feedback on your writing. It links you to publishers and lets you sample a range of current magazines both in Britain and America. You can use it to visit the homepages of famous writers, universities, and writer's groups, and sample their latest work. It can give you news about writers' grants, festivals, fellowships and competitions. You can mail what would otherwise be bulky manuscripts cheaply and safely. Most importantly, the web has given rise to a new way of writing that might alter the very conventions and ideas that this book as a whole has been discussing.

But first you need to know how to use it.

SEARCH ENGINES

There is a huge range of material on the web, and a search engine is a computer programme designed to help you sift it. Among the most popular are:

Altavista	www.altavista.digital.com
Ask Jeeves	www.askjeeves.com
Excite	www.excite.com
Lycos	www.lycos.com
Yahoo!	www.yahoo.com

The one you choose is a question of taste, and of its suitability for the task in hand. All the above are worth testing for speed, layout and user-friendliness. Some, like Yahoo!, have a large directory which can be useful but can also inundate you with results, giving you more than you either need or have the time to read. Ask Jeeves encourages you to pose simple questions and is a boon to the novice surfer with its clear layout and lack of jargon. It will probably tell you how to express your question more effectively, to keep your search words as concise and simple as you can, and how to use plus and minus signs.

When you have decided on your search word(s), enter them into the Text Box or Search Box where your cursor is waiting. The search engine will then explore the web for pages that contain these words, and return the Search Results with a list of hypertext links to those pages. If your first attempt overwhelms you, then narrow your field by including more specific details.

Hypertext links

A hypertext link is an area of your screen which will bring up another screen if you click on it with your cursor. You may have already used one such link to connect yourself to the internet, and another to find your search engine. Hypertext links act like doors, allowing you to move from one virtual space to another.

WHAT IS HYPERTEXT FICTION?

Strictly speaking, nothing new.

The page is replaced by a screen with hypertext links to other screens, which means that the distinguished characteristic of hypertext fiction is its non-linear nature. Think of a classic plot – boy meets girl, boy loses girls, boy finds girl. Even if you complicate the story – boy, having lost girl, thinks back to the time he met girl and, as he retraces the past, he finds her again – the events still unfold in time and the reader follows the events in the order set down by the writer. Put simply, in a novel we begin at the beginning and finish at the end; or we read the first line of a poem, then the second and so on. We are guided to a conclusion.

Or are we?

There have always been writers who have chafed at this chronological straitjacket. In John Fowles' novel, *The French Lieutenant's Woman*, for instance, the author puts in several appearances, discusses possible plots and difficulties and, eventually, tossing a coin, gives us two alternative endings. In the previous century, William Thackeray has his amoral heroine, Becky Sharp, seem penitent and newly virtuous at the end of

Vanity Fair, but the last thing on the printed page is Thackeray's own illustration which has Becky leering back at us, and looking far from remorseful. First as writer and then as artist, Thackeray gives us two distinct endings, deploying image and text in a way which anticipates hypertext fiction.

Other writers have gone further. Vladimir Nabokov's *Pale Fire* is a novel in the guise of a long poem and its footnotes so that we do not read continuously but flip back and forth between the two, which, more often than not, contradict each other. Milorad Pavic's *The Dictionary of the Khazars* can only be read like a dictionary or encyclopaedia by going from entry to entry. There are even two published versions of the novel – one male, one female – but, whichever edition is read, no two readers will experience the novel in the same way. B. S. Johnson's *The Unfortunates* is a novel that comes in a box with loose chapters. It is the reader who decides on the order in which they are read.

Think about how *you* read even the most traditional fiction. Are you always passive in the face of a novel, or do you sometimes skip bits, or dip in and out? Do you finish the book in one sitting, reading every word, or do you sometimes flick forward to see what happens, or back to remind yourself of a certain scene or character?

Hypertext fictions develop this subversive approach, playing games with the relationship between text, writer and reader in new and liberating ways. They also break down established divisions. The page is replaced by a four-dimensional space to which animation, music-making, video and DVD software can all contribute, with conventions becoming increasingly fluid and playful.

WHAT NEXT?

Using software like Storyspace to create the links and spaces, you can write your own hypertext fiction. The 'spaces' can hold words, images, animation, video and sound. You can link these spaces to create a narrative, using guard fields to influence or block a reader's progress, or draw them in a certain direction. Crucially, the reader should almost always be allowed a choice; not only should the narrative possibilities multiply, but also the reader's power to determine them. Point of view, closure, structure, time itself become playthings for the mutual pleasure of the writer and the reader.

Imagine this is the opening page of a hypertext fiction.

John
In the only photograph I have of her she is gazing into the camera as if it were her best friend. A man in a dark jacket has his arms about her and his face nuzzles her neck as if it has found a home there. Her wide skirt balloons in the breeze. Behind them, the promenade, the sand, the sea.

It is August Bank Holiday, 1930.

I tell people it is my grandmother but Ada was not my grandmother. The photograph was found, after her death, by a cleaner in the nursing home.

The cleaner, Claire, left shortly after. She married, was childless and drifted into fostering.

I am the one child she adopted.

This is the sequence as I know it. It is about only being loosely, accidentally connected. We make patterns out of life so that we can fool ourselves into believing we understand it. I'm not sure if there is a pattern to my life, or Claire's or Ada's, and I'm not sure if I'd understand it if there was.

At the bottom of this page there will be three hypertext boxes entitled Ada, Claire, John. As a reader you will have a choice as to whose story or 'pattern' you wish to hear next. Click on Ada and you will be linked to a space where, perhaps, Ada tells us what happened in the photograph. Click on Claire and you might be linked to the scene in which, as a cleaner, she first finds the photograph. Click on John – and who knows what? It will probably contradict whatever we learn from Ada or Claire. At the end of whichever page or space you chose, there will be more choices, more characters, more ways in which the story can be told, consumed, navigated, understood. Instead of walking the straight path of conventional fiction, you will have entered a labyrinth.

As you have seen, this kind of thing has already been done in book form, but in this hypertext fiction you could have the photograph itself. You could click on the photograph and animate it. You could have John speak to you. You could have music, a soundtrack. The text could be superimposed on the photograph. The sea could move behind it, wave after wave. You could summon the sound of the surf, a distant fairground, Ada laughing and happy, or have Claire whisper throughout, 'John is a liar. Don't believe him.' Can you do this in a book?

EXPLORING

You do not need to be a computer expert to explore hypertext fiction. You need only to access the internet and you will find a vast new library waiting for you. Here is a list of some current examples. Hunt them down and experience them for yourself.

Eastgate

The hypertexts on a site called Eastgate all use Storyspace, which is a popular programme designed for creating complex narratives for Windows or Macintosh. They are generally on CD-ROM. All the others cited below are freely available on the internet, sometimes as excerpts. As you access them – and most have links to similar sites and projects – you will become aware of the many possibilities open to the writer.

* Eastgate Systems inc.
  http://www.eastgate.com
  The leader in the field and an excellent website: friendly, accessible, informative and inspiring. If you become more interested in this field, then many on this list will come to seem essential texts. Eastgate also has an excellent catalogue and provides regular news-letters, information on workshops and online courses, and a site that should be bookmarked and returned to regularly. Its editor, Mark Bernstein, recommends the following texts because they are gaining a historical importance, are interesting examples of hypertext fictions in their own right and because so much secondary literature discusses them.
* Michael Joyce, *Afternoon, a story*
  Often referred to as the first classic hypertext fiction, it is mentioned whenever this subject is discussed. Michael Joyce's writing mixes poetry, prose, music and design. You can find out more on his home-page at Vassar College, which often showcases his work as a writer, teacher and critic of hypertext fiction.
* Stuart Moulthrop, *Victory Garden*
  Described as a maze of connected lives overlaying media coverage of the Gulf War, this is a complex and fascinating work.
* Shelley Jackson, *Patchwork Girl*
  A love story and a feminist retelling of Mary Shelley's *Frankenstein*.
* Tim McLaughlin, *Notes Toward Absolute Zero*
  An Arctic quest, love, loss and postage stamps.
* Judy Malloy, *Its name was Penelope*
  A good example of the way hypertext fiction lends itself to prose poetry.
* Judy Malloy and Cathy Marshall, *Forward Anywhere*
  A joint work, epistolary in structure and a good example of how hypertext fiction can be an interaction between writers as well as readers.

Other inventive sites

* *253* – http://www.ryman-novel.com/
  Greg Ryman's *253* details the journey of 253 passengers on a Bakerloo line tube train. This is freely available on the web and it is as witty and as complex yet as accessible a work as any available. Ryman is a very fine writer and *253* has most of the qualities of conventional fiction – a fine style, wit and pathos, and a perceptive

take on character – but it also shows what hypertext fiction can do. Not only are the narrative potentials endless, but also you are invited to add to the story or stories – a regular feature of hypertext fiction. Make 253 the first stop on your journey and you will find yourself returning to it again and again.

- Alt-X Online Publishing Network – http://www.altx.com
  Tagged as 'where the digerati meets the literati', this site offers an excellent book review section, links to other hypertext fiction sites, and access not only to Mark Amerika's internet column but also the following site.
- The Grammatron Project – http://www.grammatron.com.
  This hypertext fiction is adventurous and eye-catching and worth a visit see what happens when video, sound and animation play as much a part in a fiction as a text.
- The Electric Chronicles – http://atnetweb.com/projects/ahneed/first.html
  Imagine the twentieth century re-imagined by future archaeologists. Created by Adrienne Wortzel, this is a bewitching work and a pleasure for the eyes.
- Heart of the Dreaming – http://www.qnet.com
  Haunting images, fascinating maps, dreamscapes and lyrical texts. Night-time reading?
- Hyperizons – http://www.duke.edu~mshumate/index.html
  This has some fine examples of hypertext fiction with many links to other sites. It is clear, well designed and jargon-free. It also has a sense of humour and a fresh, reader-friendly approach.
- Intelligent Agent – http://www.intelligentagent.com
  A literary magazine offering reviews, hypertext websites.
- New River – http://ebbs.english.vt.edu/olp/newriver/
  A very readable hypertext journal of fiction, poetry and visual art. It is edited by Edward Falco, whose *A Dream of Demons* is available from Eastgate.
- trAce – http://trace.ntu.ac.uk.
  Founded at Nottingham Trent University, this site hosts samples of hypertext fiction.

Courses and workshops

Hypertext has proliferated at an amazing speed, so this chapter cannot be definitive. Technology advances. Websites date or go out of use. New software appears with increasing frequency, enhancing the ways in which you as a writer can use the web.

For information about online workshops and courses, first try Eastgate's directory: http://www.eastgate.co/Course.html

Bookmarks or favourites

Remember to keep any useful sites or pages by clicking on either Bookmarks or Favourites and selecting 'Add Bookmark' or 'Add Favourite'. Then, if you need to revisit a site or a page, you can simply click on Bookmarks or Favourites to summon it to your screen.

DESIGNING YOUR OWN WEBSITE

If you have access to the internet you should think seriously about developing a personal website. It can be a shop window for your own work and who knows who will pass by? Most computers come with software that allows you to design a homepage, and your internet server may also encourage you to create one. Instructions are simple to follow, and you will find no difficulty in creating a page that announces your existence to the virtual world. You can often download examples freely from the net – use your search engine to locate them. There are even companies which will design a website for you.

Keep the initial page (or homepage) neat and simple in its design, and text to a minimum. You will be offered a riot of colours and may end up with a page that inspires only migraines. Hypertext allows you layer upon layer of pages or spaces, so on this page you can offer access to your poetry, stories, or latest scripts by creating a list of hypertext links for clicking. There is no limit to what you can include: e-mail addresses, a chat room, work in progress or text for others to comment upon or develop. Your website exists not only to advertise and publish your work, but also to create new work or hypertext fiction.

Further reading

Not surprisingly given the issues it raises, the world wide web has already generated a great deal of secondary material. Many magazines such as *The Writer's News* run regular features on electronic writing. *Online Guardian* (published Thursdays) is also useful. For the beginner, helpful introductions in book form include *The Guardian Guide to the Internet* and Angus J. Kennedy's *The Internet: The Rough Guide*. For ideas about creating your own hypertext fiction you could also read Steve Birkett's *The Gutenberg Elegies* (Faber and Faber, London, 1994).

CONCLUSION

For writers who bemoan the lack of outlets, the internet offers a whole new market. Eastgate Inc. are, at present, leaders in the field, but most of the websites listed above appear to welcome submissions, and there are many competitions and prizes. In May 1997 the New York University Press Electronic Media established a $1,000 prize to encourage new work. They can be accessed on http:www.nyupress.nyu.edu/edit.html

The world wide web is a phenomenon which belongs to all of us. You can be part of the evolution of this exciting and important new development, so be ready to take advantage of the opportunities it offers. There is a virtual universe waiting for you.

15 WRITING FROM RESEARCH
Dymphna Callery

'A writer who omits things because he does not know them only makes hollow places in his writing.'[1]

Ernest Hemingway

INTRODUCTION

Research is finding out what we do not know and more about what we think we know. All writers have to do research, unless they work in the sphere of pure fantasy. It is part of the creative process. Developing a nose for interesting material will keep your writer's journal full of ideas for future use, and mean that you will never be stuck for 'something to write about'.

Research may involve searching out material in libraries, or through agencies, but it is also the necessary art of close observation and careful listening. Whether the source is encyclopaedias or real life, the material still has to be shaped and crafted to maintain the reader's interest.

GETTING STARTED

Hemingway maintained that seeing and listening were the two fundamental attributes necessary to the writer. Your raw material is essentially the study of human beings, their relationships to each other, to the world and what goes on around them. As it says in Chapter 1, 'Observation and discovery', your eyes and ears are your basic research tools.

Writers need to cultivate their natural curiosity: 'the arts of observing without seeming to observe and of probing without seeming to probe are skills that can – and should – be acquired'.[2] This means learning to listen to others rather than thinking of what you are going to say next, and sharpening your observation skills.

Practice will develop your skills in note taking and interviewing. You can be inspired by real events, television programmes, your family history or newspaper articles. Note any items which interest you in your writing journal, or cut them out and stick them in. But note also why you were interested and what you feel about the items. Your passion for a subject will not only drive your research but will also infuse your writing, ultimately making it more gripping for the reader.

Watching

Watch any simple activity, such as a football game, or someone cooking a meal. Remember what the sounds were and anything said as well as how it looked, where it took place, how people entered into the activity, any smells or sensations. Notice where any action gives the participant(s), or you as the watcher, a sense of excitement. Wait a few hours, then write it down. Come back to it the next day and see whether you have captured the essence of the activity, or if it is crowded with details. Be critical. Redraft it so that a reader might get the same feeling from it as you did from watching. Try reworking it from the perspective of someone involved in the activity.

BACKGROUND RESEARCH

Whatever medium you are working in, it is not always possible to rely on personal experience or imagination and you will need to consult second-hand sources. Consider what you might need to know to develop either of the pieces above: knowledge of the rules of football, for example, or culinary expertise. It is important to get your facts right. Writers who do not lose credibility with the reader. Correct details ground the reader, ensuring that they trust the writer. Background research can be divided into four categories:

* geographical (which may involve visiting places or consulting maps)
* historical (which involves checking appropriate sources)
* procedural (which involves contacting 'insiders' and consulting documentation)
* technical (which may involve checking manuals or other relevant sources).

Ken Loach's film *Land and Freedom*, for example, is about British men who went to fight in the Spanish Civil War and he had to research the landscape, the historical records (including first-hand written accounts and interviews with survivors), documents referring to army procedures and technical information about the weapons used. Crime writers invariably have contacts in the police force with whom they check both procedural and technical data.

Your first port of call is the reference section of a library which houses encyclopaedias and directories. Do not be shy about asking a librarian for advice. They are trained professionals who know where to look for even the most obscure item, whether it be a cricketing score from the West Indies in 1956 or the number of whales killed in the last five years. Getting to know your way round your local or university library – how the books are organized, where the periodicals are kept, how to access back copies of newspapers, etc. – is time well spent.

The internet is a wonderful resource. To use it effectively, without undue time-wasting, you need to be sure of your key words. The more specific the title of your search, the more relevant the information will be. Planning your research when you have a particular subject in mind, and keeping accurate records of, for example, the websites you have visited, are part of the writing process. Use your writer's journal rather than the back of an envelope. Storing data and references on disk is not only sensible, it helps you to view research in a professional manner. Get the *Radio Times* every week, and search it for material you may wish to record. Never ignore serendipity.

RESEARCH AS A PRIMARY SOURCE

Factual information can be a springboard for the imagination. There are many examples of research as the primary source in all forms of writing. In Roger McGough's collection, *Defying Gravity*, the poems on natural elements illuminate scientific principles. Lynda La Plante bases many of her screenplays on real stories bought from members of the criminal underworld. *Captain Corelli's Mandolin* is based on Louis de Bernières' research into the conflict between Greece and Italy in the Second World War. He also makes effective use of his knowledge of music and mandolin playing.

To use research as a starting point, you need to utilize your writer's journal as an ideas bank, which might contain:

- newspaper articles
- family history
- photographs: places, people
- maps
- website addresses
- postcards: places, people, historical reproductions
- historical events that interest you
- photocopies of articles on your pet subject
- quotations from individuals.

This list is not prescriptive. Be guided by your own curiosity and interests. But be alert to what is going on around you also. Remember always to cite your sources in case you need to go back to them at some point for clarification.

View research as an investment in your creative potential, for it is in a general sense the fuel for writing. In the specific sense, where a particular event, story or period is the substance of a piece, you need to gather as much material as you need to feel confident about transposing it into fictional terms. This means tracking down material. A sound knowledge of available sources is essential, and the best starting point is Ann Hoffmann's book, *Research for Writers*, which covers just about every aspect of research from checking technical data to tracing contemporary accounts of events, and includes addresses for specialist libraries and agencies. Sheila Yeger's *The Sound of One Hand Clapping* contains an inspirational chapter on research based on her own experiences as a playwright, and the insights she offers are applicable to any writing medium.

Whereas a researcher's prime goal is the acquisition of information, the writer's task is to shape that information in a way that gives pleasure, to entertain as well as enlighten. Your task is not to parade knowledge. Rather, you need to have absorbed it so that it becomes an invisible thread in your work.

Rewriting the news

Take an account of a recent event as recorded in a newspaper, or on broadcast news, that intrigues you. Rewrite the item in fictional or poetic form. How closely do you need to stay to the original item? What happens if you change characters' names or location? Try redrafting the piece from a first-person narrative. How effective is this?

DOCUMENTARY NARRATIVE

Documentary narratives have become fashionable in recent times, notably Thomas Keneally's *Schindler's Ark*, which was made into the film *Schindler's List*. Controversy has arisen over whether such works should be described as history, reportage, non-fiction novels, 'faction' or 'new journalism'. This last phrase was coined by Tom Wolfe, who saw himself as the pioneer of a new form. He felt writers were neglecting contemporary social reality and that the task of the novelist was to recognize, and write about, what was going on around them, as he had done in his book *Radical Chic*.

It is worth remembering that the novel form grew from early journalism, Daniel Defoe's *Journal of the Plague Year* being a seminal example. But notice too how modern journalism imitates the fiction writer's concern with narrative, character and detail. Television is particularly prone to blurring the line between reality and fiction with the hybrid form of the 'docudrama', for example, where real events are dramatized and presented in the same manner as fictional stories.

The guarantee that a story is 'true' can override considerations of form and crafting. It is easy to get caught up in the research process and forget that the research is the starting point and not the goal. There is an important dividing line between being a 'nerd' and acquiring information. As a fiction writer you are working *from* and *with* research. The creative process is just as crucial as when working from your imagination. However fascinating the material, ultimately it is the way you shape it which counts.

Specific techniques useful in transposing research into documentary narrative are:

- translating summaries of events into 'scenes'[3]
- putting reported speech into dialogue
- changing an impersonal point of view into that of 'characters', i.e. individual perspectives.

Using such techniques injects the material with more immediacy, creating the effect that the reader is witnessing or eavesdropping on an event.

HISTORICAL RESEARCH

Engaging with historical research means working like an actor improvising from given material: putting yourself in the position of the people involved in a situation and imagining what it was like. For this you need a reservoir of knowledge about the individuals and the period. You will not use all the research material directly, but it will inform your writing.

Published texts are a major accessible source, but be aware that there may be more than one 'authority' on a particular period. Back copies of national newspapers are held in Britain at the British Library and in the USA at the Library of Congress, although you need a reader's ticket, usually by prior application. Public libraries often keep back copies of local papers. The Public Records Office in Kew is a favourite haunt of writers, with its records of parish registers, schools, and births and deaths going back several centuries. You can write to them, but visiting may stimulate you in unexpected ways. Graveyards offer the writer a great deal, not least a fund of names. In the USA the National Archives and Records Administration internet site can be accessed on http://www.naragov. and state and county offices will hold information, although access may be restricted by the legal constraints of the Federal Privacy Act.

In addition to finding out the relevant facts concerning a historical event, you will also find it helpful to investigate the social and cultural context so that manners, customs and daily life are credible. To build a visual picture for yourself you will find visiting museums invaluable. There you can see furniture, artefacts and clothes that have been used and worn. Art galleries display paintings and sculpture which capture the *zeitgeist* of particular eras. You do not need to overload yourself with historical detail, but absorbing information in this interactive way may help you feel familiar with the world you are creating.

BIOGRAPHICAL RESEARCH

Biographical material can be used to write formal and authoritative texts on celebrities past and present, but there are numerous examples of 'fictional' accounts of famous people in poetry and plays as well as in the novel. If you are fascinated by a particular figure you need to find out everything about them. The process is similar to historical research. The *Dictionary of National Biography* is a comprehensive work of reference, and Ann Hoffmann's book contains a helpful chapter on sources for biographical research. More informally, Sheila Yeger suggests that handling something once touched by the person can inspire you in quite a different way from reading about them.[4] Similarly, visiting where they lived or walked, or spending time with someone who practises the same trade, will enable you to pick up clues for creating their world. Getting to 'know' them may also mean consulting the letters, writings or thoughts of those who knew them.

It is important to remember that you are not reporting on a world which exists, so your interpretation is more important than the 'official' view. Nor are you writing an academic essay or journalistic piece. You are *interpreting* a life and using the information imaginatively to create something new.

THE HORSE'S MOUTH

People and places are a great resource. If your story or drama is set on a fishing boat, research on the spot will prove far more useful than reading a book. If you want to write about drug smuggling, ask to visit a Customs and Excise operation. TV writers regularly go to observe the medical and police worlds around which their stories revolve. Through interactive research you pick up on things in a different way. Research is part of the creative process and how your discoveries affect you is an important element. You will learn most by keeping your thoughts to yourself and letting others go about their work and do the talking.

INTERVIEWING

Interviewing is a skill acquired through practice. Preparation is essential. Your interview will be more productive if you have a list of questions, although you need to be open to what your interviewee wants to say. Your aim is to get the maximum information from people, and they are usually more forthcoming if they feel relaxed. Taping conversations is the best method, as you will often forget key points, or find yourself concentrating on writing down what people say instead of listening to them. However, some people are nervous of being recorded and the machine may inhibit them. Try getting them relaxed in a friendly manner first and then ask if you can record the conversation. Saving your 'key' question until towards the end of the interview is a good ploy, so that you ease the person in.

Always be honest about your motives and treat any information sensitively. Your sources will be justified in feeling angry and abused if you have misrepresented them or made fun of their emotions and vulnerability.

AN ETHICAL NOTE

Your passion for your subject will colour your interpretation of the facts, and although it is important to write in your own voice, if you are not careful you may find you are delivering propaganda and are in danger of alienating your reader. Writing to persuade requires a sound grasp of the opposition. To present a valid case for vegetarianism, for example, may involve researching how animals are slaughtered and offering an informed view of a carnivore's perspective.

Although many writers claim that they draw on relations and friends as source material, there is an ethical question here. Hemingway stated that he had 'a wonderful novel to write about Oak Park and would never do it because I did not want to hurt living people'.[5] Transposing material into fiction requires a sensitive attitude and you should be sure about your motives for using material from those close to you. It is best to ask permission to use someone's story and be honest about why it appeals to you.

Writers have always lifted raw material from other media. Shakespeare and his contemporaries regularly raided the penny broadsheets for salacious tales, and his 'history plays' are an early example of writing from historical research. The ethics of taking factual events and weaving fictional stories around them, as in the historical novel and the 'biopic', seem to depend on the distance of time: the closer we are to an actual event the more we seem to demand truth; the further away it is, the more poetic licence we allow. Yet sometimes it is the poetic vision of the writer which shapes the material to allow the reader or spectator to gain an insight into a deeper, human truth as opposed to mere verisimilitude.

CONCLUSION

When you are engaged in research, allow yourself time to browse, because you never know what you might find. Build a research library which includes relevant dictionaries, a concise encyclopaedia, and books on your special subjects. Bookmark useful sites on the web.

Above all, take time to digest useful information; otherwise your writing will be dominated by the process rather than fuelled by it. Research is there to be enjoyed as part of the adventure of becoming a writer.

Notes

1 Ernest Hemingway, *Death in the Afternoon* (first published 1938; repr. Penguin, Harmondsworth, 1966).
2 Ann Hoffmann, *Research for Writers*, 4th edn (A. and C. Black, London, 1992).
3 Hoffmann, *Research*.
4 Sheila Yeger, *The Sound of One Hand Clapping: A Guide to Writing for the Theatre* (Amber Lane Press, Oxford, 1990).
5 Letter to Charles Fenton quoted in *Ernest Hemingway on Writing*, ed. by Larry Phillips (Granada, London, 1984).

16 REDRAFTING AND EDITING

Jenny Newman

'Anyone can write – and almost everyone you meet these days is writing. However, only the writers know how to rewrite. It is this ability alone that turns the amateur into a pro.'[1]

INTRODUCTION

As a writer you need time for inspiration, for getting in touch with your unconscious. Your first draft is a good place for going out on a limb, for fathoming new feelings, or trying out a fresh tone of voice without being monitored. This may mean shutting out your inner censor (Virginia Woolf called hers 'the Angel in the House') and letting yourself write as unselfconsciously, freely and fluently as you can.

But the creative process needs more than inspiration. As Tolstoy put it, 'In a writer there must always be two people – the writer and the critic.'[2] At a certain point you must draw a line under what you have written, put it in your desk drawer, and groom the dog or make a pot of tea or start a new project. The longer you can bring yourself to leave your first draft to one side without looking at it, the better, but a week – or even a day or two – is far preferable to no time at all.

If you are a student, you may be writing to a tight schedule. Try, all the same, to leave yourself time to re-read and amend your work before handing it in. If you write on a word processor, print out your work before you revise. Reading a screen is hard on the eye, so mistakes are easier to miss than they are on paper. Or, if you have grown word blind, record your work and listen through headphones while you go for a walk or do the chores. This is the first step towards becoming your own editor or, rather, editors, because the all-important process of revision has several steps.

Throughout this chapter, 'to redraft' means to revise in the more comprehensive, thoroughgoing way typical of the early stages of the revision process, and 'to edit' means to pay close attention to detail and fine tuning when the work is nearing completion.

REAL WRITING IS REWRITING

The extra effort in redrafting that you may, in the beginning, find tedious is precisely that which will make your work gripping to read, hear or see. It can be fun, too, as a better version starts taking shape. Only an inexperienced writer dumps his work on someone else's desk for the final, crucial review, the one that often makes the difference between success and failure, acceptance and rejection.

To rewrite is to become a good parent to your work, seeing it through all the stages of its development. Checking facts, looking for spelling mistakes, clichés, and repetition, or fiddling with commas and semi-colons is only part of it. During revision you learn new techniques, tackle problems of structure, and uncover the meaning of your work – which is why one rewrite is seldom enough.

Interviewer:	How much rewriting do you do?
Hemingway:	It depends. I rewrote the ending to *Farewell to Arms*, the last page of it, thirty-nine times before I was satisfied.
Interviewer:	Was there some technical problem there? What was it that had stumped you?
Hemingway:	Getting the words right.

When you are struggling to 'get the words right'[3] do not overlook your potential readers. You may already be in a workshop group with ground rules for considering draft material (if not, see Chapter 3, 'The workshop'). Or you may already have trusted readers on whose opinion you depend. It is now that they come in useful, not when the work is burnished and comma perfect. Remember also that you are in charge, and may have an overview that they cannot share.

REVISING FOR MEANING

This is the most involving, demanding and important form of revision, and may be partly a question of trusting your intuition. Contrary to popular belief, the meaning of what you write is not necessarily something you start with; nor does it always pop fully formed into your first draft. Flannery O'Connor is only one of many who talk about the process of writing as an act of discovery.[4] Meaning may take shape over several drafts; or you may, halfway through, have a nagging sense that something has been left unsaid, without knowing quite what it is. Raymond

Carver feels that his revisions take him slowly into the heart of what the story is about. 'If the writing cannot be made as good as it is within us to make it, then why do it? In the end, the satisfaction of having done our best, and the proof of that labour, is the one thing we can take into the grave.'[5] Revision, he believes, is about refusing to settle for less than the best you can do.

Finding your window

When you think you have finished, ask yourself the question, 'What is my poem, script or story about?' And then ask yourself, 'What is it really about?' If you cannot respond briefly and lucidly, it may be a sign that you need to spend more time clarifying your subject matter to yourself. Do as Stanley Elkin suggests, and 'after five or six drafts, write what [your] story means in one sentence. Then use that sentence to cut, revise, add, adjust, or change the next drafts. Use that sentence as a filter, or a window, to the whole piece.'[6]

REVISING FOR CHARACTER

The novelist Sue Gee says that character is all. Certainly readers and viewers like vigorous, well-drawn story people. Often this stage in revision means listening to your misgivings. You may sense, for instance, that your characters are not as compelling as they could be, but be unable to see why. This section is *not* a formula for when you write, or to be taken as proof that your story is lacking; it is simply a series of points for you to ponder.

If your heroine obstinately refuses to come to life, you may not have clarified what she wants. And have you got a good antagonist to stop her getting it? Consider giving her a detailed past, even if it does not all appear in the script or the story. Knowing a person's history alters your understanding of who she is today. Imagine your response to a loudmouth at a party – until you hear that she has just come from three years in solitary confinement.

Young writers in particular are prone to set their dramas in student flats. Why not give your character some kind of employment? You could base it on a job of your own, or research a likely career (books on work make compelling reading) or else hang around somebody else's workplace, taking notes (see Chapter 1, 'Observation and discovery'). Your character's work can shape his perceptions, and give you a store of unusual metaphors for his vision of experience.

Many writers secretly feel that their characters are their slaves.

Nevertheless, to the reader the characters must look as though they are driving the action. Do your characters wait like puppets to be jerked into life, or do they quarrel with each other, fall in love, gossip behind each other's backs, try and stop each other from getting what they want, from a variety of motives, good and bad? When you are redrafting, scrutinize them all in terms of function: protagonist, antagonist, lover, child, stepmother, victim, or a bit of local colour. Have they all got something to do? If they double up, can they be cut? Or, alternatively, is there a character missing?

Few stories or scripts have space to develop every character, so many writers depend on stereotypes (the unflappable nurse, the bossy teacher) for the walk-on roles that the viewer or reader needs to recognize quickly. But if your main character is a dumb body builder, or a wily East End barrow boy, your reader may feel that she knows him already, and lose her wish to read on. You may, of course, enjoy overturning such stereotypes, as Anita Brookner does through her novelist-heroine in *Hotel du Lac*.

Whether the character is major or minor, check that the dialogue is taut and well-constructed, and that it serves a purpose besides conveying information.[7] Try and give all your characters distinct voices and speech patterns. And do not call your two main characters Harry and Henry. Distinctive names beginning with different letters will help your reader keep track of who is who.

REVISING FOR PACE

There is no one way to pace a piece of writing. Chekhov suggested that you write a beginning, middle and end, then cut the beginning and the end.[8] Dangerous advice, perhaps – but if you have read Chekhov's stories you may see some of its advantages. Many script writers have likewise proposed that you enter your scene as late as possible, and leave it as early as you can, as has the short story writer Raymond Carver ('Get in, get out. Don't linger. Go on').[9] When you revisit that crucial beginning, ask yourself if your story starts too slowly. In the first draft, openings are often just 'throat-clearing' and can be scrapped at a later stage; or else they can be redrafted, or even written at the very end.

If you sense that the structure sags in the middle, ask if the line through your story is clear. If in doubt, try writing it out in one paragraph, and see if anything has been left out. Is the conflict and tension sustained? Do you have the right balance between dialogue and action? Scripts, novels and short stories can all be ruined by too many 'talking heads'. List your main plot points and check that they are in the right order (i.e. going from smaller to larger, with cause followed by effect). Do they hinge on a need or desire in the mind of your central character? Is there enough at stake?

You can always tighten a story by 'putting a clock on it' – think of *High Noon* or *Silence of the Lambs* or any other film or book which kept you on the edge of your seat with its race against time. Such plots are not weighed down by too much flashback, especially early on; nor are there too many subplots to detract from the main action. Yet every reader or viewer needs the occasional breather. Fiction writers know many methods – such as description, or the use of retrospect – of slowing the pace. Even the tensest film script should be spiked with scenes which vary the rhythm, by focusing, for example, on atmosphere or character development.

Every piece of writing has its own momentum, and after the struggle to get started, and plot the middle, you may find that the last third is downhill all the way. This is why it is tempting to rush. But the stronger the story, the more your reader or viewer will feel cheated if you skimp on the turning point and resolution. Ask yourself if anything has changed. Most importantly, has your protagonist learnt something, whether pleasing or painful?

Placing the final full stop is always a delicate matter. If the ending feels hurried, ask yourself if the climax comes out of nowhere, or is it brought about by your main character? Does it have an internal logic, following on from your previous plot points?

On the other hand, if your finale seems flat, see if you have written past your ending, and given your reader not one but two conclusions.

REVISING FOR STYLE

The poet and the scriptwriter are opposites. The poet redrafts in solitude, and can make the amendments which please him, down to the last semicolon. If a poem is altered without his permission by, say, a magazine editor, he will have a right to complain. A poet may not be paid much, but over his work he reigns supreme.

A writer for a television soap is part of a team. For her, revision can mean letting a script go: to script editors who prune and alter it, to producers, directors and eventually to actors. Writing for TV is not a solitary but a collaborative act.

Yet these diverse writers share one key belief: that each word counts. This is why both must revise ruthlessly. For the poet, the medium's intensity means that he must weigh every word, test every image, scrutinize his use of metre and his line endings. The short story writer too may take as much care as the poet. The screenwriter, on the other hand, may not share such scrupulous attention to detail; yet she is up against limits of time, space and the production business, where every word costs money, and must therefore have maximum impact. Both kinds of writer must learn how to 'murder their darlings'.

Few writers in any medium find that good style happens by accident: it develops little by little from your first rough notes to your final version. Jeanette Winterson uses the analogy of the acrobat: years of practice go into one single, seemingly effortless movement. Your goal is not to make writing effortless, but to make it look effortless. Underline your first interesting line or sentence. If it is not the first one, or very near it, why not?

Surplus words and phrases are not just an extra your reader can choose to discard. They detract from your whole style, and leech the life even from those words that are well chosen.

In particular, watch out for creative minefields:

- overkill, such as lists of adjectives; or laying on so many details that you lessen credibility. Chekhov believed it was an insult to over-describe; the writer should give just enough detail to evoke the reader's knowledge of life.[10] Elmore Leonard says, 'I try to leave out the parts that people skip',[11] which is another way of saying that in writing less often means more. Sometimes you need the guts to cut.
- showing off at your reader's expense. Aim at being straightforward and exact, rather than too high-flown.
- predictable noun-adjective combinations such as 'bitter pill' or 'clear blue sky'.
- overuse of adverbs. A strong, expressive verb, such as 'drift', 'mooch' or 'slouch' may be more telling than 'walk slowly'. Or, rather than *telling* us that your hero reads incessantly, *show* us his red-rimmed eyes.
- redundant words, as in the following phrases: 'appreciate in value', 'rack and ruin', 'hope for the future', 'I personally'. Compile your own list of surplus expressions.
- fussy, overcomplicated punctuation.
- meaningless terms such as 'in point of fact', 'at the end of the day' and 'lo and behold'.
- weak intensifiers such as very, really, extremely and exceptionally.
- overworked similes ('green as grass') and metaphors ('dyed in the wool').
- misattributions, such as 'she clutched the receiver in one hand, while with the other she nibbled a sandwich' (with the tiny teeth in her palm?).

REVISING FOR ACCURACY

Theatres, magazines, production companies and publishing houses are bombarded with submissions from would-be writers. Who would struggle to read a badly laid-out script, or choose an ill-punctuated, misspelt novel over one which is comma perfect? Attention to detail suggests a professionalism and pride in your work which goes well beyond mere pedantry.

In an Isaac Babel short story the narrator says, 'No iron can pierce the heart with such force as a period put in just the right place.'[12] Punctuation is an aspect of meaning, telling your reader how your sentences are paced, and clarifying the rhythm of your prose. In poetry it creates vital tension, overriding or corroborating your line length and stanza form. If you are unsure of the rules, find a recent edition of G. V. Carey's *Mind the Stop*[13] and keep it on your desk.

Always check your facts. If you misspell a street name in Harare, or your character's flight out of Gander is delayed by snow at the wrong time of year, you may lose the confidence of your readers or audience. Consult Chapter 15, 'Writing from research', for sources of information, and build a collection of reference books on the areas you write about, plus *The Oxford Dictionary for Writers and Editors*,[14] a good thesaurus, and a dictionary. The complete *Oxford English Dictionary* will soon be available on the web at most good libraries, where it will be regularly updated, or you may, if you wish, become a subscriber yourself.

IN CONCLUSION

Be methodical about keeping your drafts. If you use a word processor, copy your work each time you start to rewrite, and print out regularly; otherwise you will be left with only one version, and no record of how you reached it. It is possible to revise too much, and knowing when to stop takes practice. Sometimes first thoughts are best thoughts, and later drafts can lose conviction and freshness. But more new writers stop too soon than go on too long.

Notes

1 William C. Knott, quoted in Janet Burroway, *Writing Fiction: A Guide to Narrative Craft*, 4th edn. (HarperCollins, New York, 1996).
2 *Talks with Tolstoi*, ed. by A. B. Goldenveizer (1922), trans. S. S. Koteliansky and Virginia Woolf (1923), quoted in Miriam Allott, *Novelists on the Novel* (Routledge, London, 1968).
3 Quoted in Bernays and Painter (eds.), *What If? Writing Exercises for Fiction Writers*, revised and expanded edn. (HarperCollins College Publishers, London, 1995).
4 Flannery O'Connor, 'Writing Short Stories', quoted in Raymond Carver, 'On Writing', *Fires* (Picador, London, 1986).
5 Carver, *Fires*.
6 Quoted in Bernays and Painter, *What If?*
7 See Chapter 9, 'Writing for stage', and Chapter 6, 'Short story writing'.
8 Quoted in Bernays and Painter, *What If?*
9 Carver, *Fires*.
10 Quoted in Bernays and Painter, *What If?*

11 Quoted in Bernays and Painter, *What If?*
12 Quoted in Carver, *Fires*.
13 G. V. Carey, *Mind the Stop* (Cambridge University Press, Cambridge, 1939; repr. Penguin, Harmondsworth, 1976).
14 *The Oxford Dictionary for Writers and Editors* (Clarendon Press, Oxford, 1981).

17 GETTING PUBLISHED, PRODUCED OR PERFORMED

Jenny Newman,

Edmund Cusick and

Aileen La Tourette

There are no guarantees that any piece of work, however brilliant, will be what people are looking for at any given time. Success depends on a number of factors, and luck is one of them.

But there are better and worse ways of trying to place a piece of work. At the very least, you can avoid some of the mistakes which will only succeed in wasting time. Always submit your work on one side of A4 paper, double-spaced unless otherwise instructed. Do not staple the pages together or wrap each one in a plastic folder; use paper clips. Number your pages, and include the title or some of it on every page. Always include a stamped, self-addressed envelope with any submission of work, and make sure the postage is correct. Do not send off your epic novel or screenplay without making a phone call and finding out a name – not of a company, or a network, but the name of an individual – to send it to; and checking whether it might be better to send a treatment for the screenplay. It is usually better to send a synopsis and several chapters rather than a whole novel. Always send a covering letter saying a bit about yourself, and detailing, briefly, any other work you have had published, produced or performed. Once you have sent what is required (keeping a record of what you sent and where and when you sent it) try to forget about it. The best of all possible therapies for the inevitable waiting period is to embark on a new piece of work.

Pay attention to the response you get when your work is returned. There is not much you can learn from a rejection slip, but sometimes an editor will scribble a few words on it. Read them. There are degrees and stages of rejection and acceptance. Any little word of encouragement, any hint as to what might succeed with a particular editor, is something to go on.

Think about the specific market for the piece of work you are trying to sell. If it is a short story, for example, do some research into magazines which publish them. Literary magazines are expensive to buy, but the Poetry Library on London's South Bank stocks a good range of them. Your own local library will order them for you if you ask. Scour *The Writer's and Artist's Yearbook*[1] or *The Writer's Handbook*[2] for names, and then read the magazine. See if your work fits in. Keep your eye open, especially for magazines just starting up. They will be on the lookout for new writers to fill their pages.

Do not despise competitions. They can be a good way to get your creative juices flowing. There are many short story competitions each year, some run by big, glossy magazines like *Cosmopolitan* and some smaller and more local. Magazines like *Writer's News* and *The New Writer* will list competitions, and the Arts Council and regional arts boards publish comprehensive listings. Your regional arts board will have a mailing list, and it is worth ringing up and putting your name on it. They will run courses, and perhaps competitions of their own, and they will know what is going on in your area.

Try local competitions. Anything and everything that gets your work out and read, or seen, by as many people as possible is good. If you have won or been placed in a local competition, at the very least, the next time you send something out, you will have something to put in your covering letter.

You can now e-mail work to American magazines, so the process of submitting is much less cumbersome. It is worth looking at the American market. There are many more openings for short stories there than here. Again, consult *The Writer's and Artist's Yearbook* and *The Writer's Handbook* for information. There are also e-zines on the web which you might have a look at as a possible market. Some of them are very prestigious, and it is considered a real coup to have your work appear in them.

You might want to consider designing your own homepage and updating it regularly as a way of promoting and showcasing your work. Have a look at some of the writers' pages already there to get ideas and information.

If you have written a novel, you may want to approach an agent. Competition is fierce, and it can be harder to get an agent than to publish. Bear in mind that many agents keep an eye on competitions. The best of all possible worlds is obviously to have an agent phone you, rather than vice versa. Sometimes an agent will leave a big agency to start up on their own. They will be looking for new clients, so keep your eyes and ears open. Again, there are lists of agents in *The Writer's and Artist's Yearbook* and *The Writer's Handbook*. Always ring up first, always write to an individual. Send a synopsis and two or three chapters in the first instance, rather than a whole book. Always send your covering letter, including details of anything you have already had published, produced or performed, and any competitions you have won or been placed in.

If an agent or publisher sends you an interested letter but does not want the manuscript you sent them, do not give up. Agents and publishers are busy people, and any words of encouragement they give you should be taken seriously. If they say keep in touch, keep in touch. Send them the next thing you write. Keep trying.

Can you send the same material to several different people at once? This is a vexed question. The short answer is that the market is tough and you, too, must be tough. So yes, you may submit manuscripts to several agents or publishers at once. But be warned that there are some agents who will not read any material not submitted to them exclusively.

If you send your work directly to a publisher or publishers, again get names. Consult *The Writer's and Artist's Yearbook*, also *The Small Press Guide*. Look carefully at specialist and smaller publishers, and for new ones starting out. Browse in your local bookshop and see what kind of books are published by which publishers. Look at their lists, see what they like. Market research like this saves time and heartache.

Much of the advice about short stories also applies to poetry. The primary market is little magazines, and competitions are even more important to poets. Enter your work as widely as possible, and try to read the judges' work to get an idea of what they think about poetry. Some poetry-reading venues have 'open mike' sessions where people read from the floor. Look at the poetry listings in *Time Out*, or check your local press, and see where readings are being held. Showing your face at local gatherings is a good way to get to know the poetry scene where you are. There are a number of books by well-known poets with suggestions regarding publication; have a look in bookshops.

Different producers want different things when it comes to submitting screenplays or scripts for television plays or radio plays. Sometimes it is only a single page of ideas. Sometimes it is a more traditional four- or five-page treatment. Sometimes, rarely, it is a whole script. Make sure you know what the producer is looking for. Get a name by ringing Channel 4 or the BBC or the company you are submitting to. There may be someone there who will chat to you about their requirements. Do not assume you have to begin with a full-length feature film. There are competitions run by Channel 4, the BBC, the British Film Institute and the British Academy of Film and Television Arts (BAFTA) for short films. Ring them and ask them to send you information. Again, try your regional arts board and the Arts Council.

Bear in mind that sometimes local drama groups want someone to film their work. Local councils may want documentary film work done. Any work you do in film will help you to gain experience and learn your craft. Check your local paper for upcoming events and ring up to see if the organizers might like a video of the day or evening.

Plays can be performed in local church halls or above local pubs. Contact local drama groups and see if they are looking for material. Have a look at what kind of work a given theatre performs, before you send them anything. Many large theatres have studio theatres where they perform plays by less well-known playwrights. Find out where and who they are through the *Writer's and Artist's Yearbook*. There are also national and international play competitions, which the drama section of your regional arts board should know about. There may be local ones as well. Rehearsed readings are a good way to get a hearing and an audience for a new play, and are far cheaper to do than a full performance.

Be resourceful. There are other ways of promoting your work; you may even invent some yourself. There is a lot of self-publishing going on, which you may wish to investigate. Do not isolate yourself. Make sure you are getting a response to your work from your writers' group, or from friends. Writers need other writers, as the chapter on workshops points out. Create support networks for yourself and use them. We can learn from each other's successes and failures as well as from our own, and we can share our highs and lows as we go along. You may have a good spell, or a bad one, at any point in your writing career. There is no corporate ladder to climb, rung by rung. There is no career structure as such.

Celebrate your victories, however small. They mean something. Be generous with yourself. You are your own employer as well as your own employee. Take breaks when you need them. Do not work until you are drained or exhausted. Do not berate yourself if a piece of work comes back. Be sympathetic, as you would be with someone else. It sounds obvious, but we sometimes have a tendency to flagellate ourselves when we fall short of our own expectations. Keep your expectations realistic, and develop your own personal strategies for dealing with the ups and downs of a writer's life.

Notes

1 *The Writer's and Artist's Yearbook* (A. & C. Black, London, published annually).
2 *The Writer's Handbook*, ed. by Barry Turner (Macmillan, London, published annually).

Conclusion

You will not become a famous writer – or a writer at all – instantly. It will take time, and there will be frustrations along the way. Most writers learn to live with a certain amount of rejection. The important thing is to keep writing and to keep pushing your work out when it and you are ready.

You have read the advice in this book, and tried out the techniques. But never be afraid to develop your own methods, and always work at your own pace. Do not rush your writing. It deserves the best chance you can give it.

Above all, do not be discouraged. You are engaged in a creative activity which is absorbing and inspiring. The creative process itself is valuable and worthwhile, and the time you spend on it will never be wasted. If you have any talent, and persevere, you will break through eventually. Be patient, be willing to work hard, and enjoy the marvellous path you have chosen for yourself. Bon voyage!

INDEX